SMART PARENTS
IS A SERIES OF FOUR

SMART PARENTS ... *children and teenagers*

WORK-BOOKS

SMART PARENTS ... *preschoolers*
SMART PARENTS ... *children (primary school)*
SMART PARENTS ... *teenagers (high school)*

COLLABORATORS

KOBUS NEETHLING
RACHÉ RUTHERFORD
HESSIE SLABBER
HANLIE QUASS
ROLLIE SCHOEMAN
LISA ESTERHUIZEN

21 smart PARENTS

building blocks for growing up creatively in the 21st century

CREATE AN EXCITING FUTURE FOR *teenagers*

KOBUS NEETHLING
& rollie schoeman

WORKBOOK ... TEENAGERS

© 1999 Carpe Diem Books
PO Box 5801• Vanderbijlpark• 1900
Tel & fax • (016) 982-3617/8
E-mail • info@carpediem.co.za
First edition, first print 1999

ISBN 1-919818-24-3

Typesetting • Cindy van Rensburg
Translation • Susan van der Walt
Proofreading • Charles Hills
Cover design • Carpe Diem Books & John-Wesley Franklin
Printing • Creda Communications

© All rights reserved. No part of this book may be reproduced
in any form without permission in writing from the publisher.

CONTENTS

    Introduction   7

    Your child's brain profile   8

1   Parents and emotional intelligence   12

LEARNING AND STUDYING

2   Why does my child's way of learning differ from mine?   19
3   Think and Do: Learning and studying activities of teenagers   21
4   Parents can facilitate the learning process and develop the weaker preferences   27
5   Deal with difficult situations   33

THE GENERATION GAP

6   This strange creature ... my child?   37
7   Parents, their brain preferences and the generation gap ...   39
8   Dealing with curfews   42
9   Music in the teenage world   44
10   The teenager surrounded by colour   47
11   Teenager privacy   50
12   You, your teenager and duties   52
13   The pocket-money issue   54
14   The teenager and experimenting   56

TEENAGER RELATIONSHIPS

15   Relationships with the opposite sex   61
16   Parents and their reaction to these relationships   64
17   Other relationships   71

ENTREPRENEURSHIP

18	Entrepreneurship – essential in the 21st century	80
19	Parents, their brain preferences and possible reactions to the idea of entrepreneurship	83
20	The teenager's brain preferences and entrepreneurship	86
21	Think and Do: Develop a business plan	107

INTRODUCTION

Parents are the primary educators of their children – a role which will be a necessity, not a choice in the 21st century. The dramatic acceleration in the pace of all processes on this planet since the last quarter of the 20th century, severely diminished the parent's role as significant counsellor of the child.

Looking at the alarming divorce rate, teenager suicides, distribution of Aids, poverty and unemployment, a finger must be pointed very sternly at the poor education and teaching of our time. The school and educational system can, as a result of uncreative and sterile methods, certainly carry a large part of the blame, but it is time for us parents to search our own hearts and to initiate an honest quest for a new, far more efficient form of parenting.

With parents fulfilling their roles with creativity, morality and dignity, our planet will once again become a pleasant place to live and our children will grow to their full potential as unique human beings with wonderful possibilities.

> *"For life goes not backward nor tarries with yesterday. You are the bows from which your children as living arrows are sent forth."*
> — *Kahlil Gibran* —

YOUR CHILD'S BRAIN PROFILE

In the first book of the series *smart* PARENTS ... *children and teenagers* you had the opportunity to determine your parenting brain profile. It is important that you as parent should understand your profile, as your brain preferences will determine, among other things, how you will make decisions, communicate and educate. Your own brain preferences play an important role in forming those of your child. Insight into your respective preferences will lead to better understanding of the differences between people and to tolerance and greater co-operation within the family.

The following activity merely gives an indication of what your teenager's brain profile may look like. The complete Neethling Brain Profile can be drawn, but as a parent you should have quite a good idea of your child's preferences.

STEP 1

Choose from any of the four blocks the SIXTEEN descriptions most applicable to your child. *You must choose at least three from each block.*

Your sixteen choices are:
-
-
-
-
-
-
-
-
-
-
-
-
-
-
-
-

YOUR CHILD'S BRAIN PROFILE

BLOCK 1

does things very methodically and step by step
room is neat
puts away sports equipment, etc. after game or use
does not throw in the towel easily
keeps to rules with ease
will diligently practise to master new skill
always on time
talks chronologically and tells story in detail
dependable
diligent
not comfortable with change
fastidious
wants to organise things and people

BLOCK 2

very loving
comfortable with physical display of love
likes to share feelings
likes friends and fond of visiting
shows empathy for others
talks easily
inclined to become emotional
can become very enthusiastic about things
sensitive
shows feelings for others (sensitive)
sometimes very dramatic
moody, varies between joy and pessimism
likes to perform in front of people

BLOCK 3

a daydreamer
imaginative
adapts easily to change
easily becomes bored with something
often asks why and "what if" questions
wonders about the future a great deal
likes to embark on something new
room is quite chaotic
usually forgets the time
does not pay much attention to particulars
has difficulty in concentrating on one thing for a long time
artistic
engaged in various things simultaneously

BLOCK 4

seldom allows feelings to influence him
wants to do things faultlessly
can be bossy
achievement is very important
likes to analyse
looks at things realistically
handles money well
interested in technology
a stickler for correct facts
can be perfectionistic
inclined to be very critical
wants to know exactly how things work
regards it as important to know how far, how long, how deep

STEP 2

Choose from the sixteen descriptions in step 1 the eight that fit your child best and write them down in sequence of preference.

1.
2.
3.
4.

5.
6.
7.
8.

STEP 3

The four blocks represent the four quadrants:

Block 1 = L2
Block 2 = R2
Block 3 = R1
Block 4 = L1

Use the above information and complete this table:

Choice	Block	Quadrant	Score
e.g. 1st	1	L2	8
1st			8
2nd			7
3rd			6
4th			5
5th			4
6th			3
7th			2
8th			1

Totals: (each quadrant starts with a score of 4)

L1: 4 + ____ =
L2: 4 + ____ =
R2: 4 + ____ =
R1: 4 + ____ =

YOUR CHILD'S BRAIN PROFILE

STEP 4

Now determine your child's brain profile by plotting the scores on the following circle (see example).

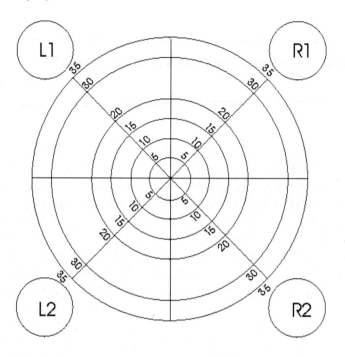

Example:

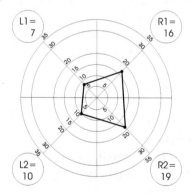

ACTIVITY

Before accepting this profile of your teenager, go through all the steps again, but now get your teenager's opinion on how he sees himself. Discuss the similarities, but especially the differences in an open, non-critical conversation and then try to compromise. You will be astonished what it reveals about your teenager. It can also be an illuminating experience for both of you.

1 PARENTS AND EMOTIONAL INTELLIGENCE

> *"Emotional intelligence is a different way of being smart."*
> – D. Goleman –

Do you as parent know what emotional intelligence is and what the shortcomings are in your emotional intelligence and that of your teenager?

Emotional intelligence (EQ) is not necessarily the opposite of IQ and one does of course possess both. Researchers of emotional intelligence have come to realize more and more that the lives of those with a high EQ are enriched by it, they are better equipped to deal with stress, they are more successful in communication and relationships and they learn life skills that lead to overall success.

The emotional experience of teenagers has been compared with a roller-coaster ride at the merry-go-round: it is just as often down as up – but never when you expect it! Because they often find the teenager's emotions so unpredictable, unexpected and incomprehensible, parents do not accept these emotions easily, disparage them, label their children as a result of these emotions and make them feel guilty and often rejected. (Read again the discussion of this subject in Book 1 – *smart* PARENTS ... *children and teenagers*, pages 70-76.)

What parents must understand, is that teenagers usually express a need through a particular emotion. Parents must therefore develop their own emotional sensitivity to be able to identify these needs in their children. It is worth the time and effort, because according to Goleman's well-known book *Emotional Intelligence*, research shows that children with a high EQ:
- learn more easily;
- have less behavioural problems;
- feel better about themselves;
- can resist peer pressure more easily;
- are less violent and more empathetic;
- can better deal with conflict;
- are happier, healthier and better achievers.

WHAT EXACTLY IS EMOTIONAL INTELLIGENCE?

It is the identification, understanding and dealing with your emotions (and those of others) in such a manner that you develop life skills and abilities which keep your thinking above the line and in this way enrich your whole life.

PARENTS AND EMOTIONAL INTELLIGENCE

Emotional intelligence can be divided into personal and social abilities.

A. PERSONAL ABILITIES

1. SELF AND PERSONAL CONSCIOUSNESS

Emotional consciousness is certainly the most important of the qualities which make up emotional intelligence. The teenager who has this ability will be able to identify, understand and control his emotions in situations. ("Control" does not necessarily mean to suppress, but to channel in positive ways.)

1) Parents can lead their teenagers to emotional consciousness by teaching them to identify their emotions:
   - Stop telling your child how he should or should not feel.
   - Help him to identify the emotion. (You feel disappointed, angry, sad, uncertain ... don't you?)
2) Parents must help their children to understand the connection between their thinking, feelings and behaviour:
   - If your child says, "Anne makes me furious" react with, for example, "I understand that you are furious (accept, identify) but you have decided (your thinking) that Anne's action was disparaging (insulting, hateful), it made you feel furious and now makes you sullen, short and impatient with everybody. Remember, you are allowed to have feelings about the behaviour of others, but you must accept responsibility for it. Is Anne's behaviour wrong? Yes, perhaps. Does Anne make you furious? No, it is your choice. Is it Anne's fault that you are behaving like this now? No, it is your choice."
   - Accept your teenager's emotions, do not condemn them, but guide them empathetically to understand that it is the way they think about situations that give rise to certain feelings and not other people.
3) Parents must make their teenagers realize that emotions influence their performance:
   - The teenager who starts the day on a wrong foot, will carry the emotional experience of the situation with him the whole day. He will be irritable, rebuff his friends and be sulky – without realizing why. His concentration will slacken, his performance will drop at different levels. Once again it is vital for the teenager to be able to identify this emotion. I am actually angry, sad, disappointed, shy. As soon as it is identified, the chances are much greater that the brain will be able to come to terms with it.
   - Teenagers who have acquired this emotional intelligence, will, in fact, convert their feelings into energy, instead of being paralysed by them. They take positive, productive action.

2. SELF-CONFIDENCE

1) Volumes have been written on this subject and there is certainly not one parent who still doubts the importance of cultivating self-confidence in his/her children. Unfortunately parents so easily miss the critical element of this self-confidence, namely: children want to feel that their parents respect them, love them, listen to them and accept them. Most teenagers know their parents love them, but do they feel it?
   - Let your teenager answer the following questions:
   My dad makes me feel he loves me (on a scale of 0-10)
   My mum makes me feel she loves me (on a scale of 0-10)
   I feel my dad loves me when _____
   I feel my mum loves me when _____
   I feel my dad doesn't love me when _____
   I feel my mum doesn't love me when _____
2) Parents must, by using emotive language, make their teenagers understand that they understand certain actions – even though they do no agree with them. ("I know how it makes you feel, I have also felt like that before.") By reacting in this way, the process of repair begins – the teenagers starts to realize that his behaviour was wrong, but his mum or dad does not reject him for it. This builds self-confidence.
   - Parents who use threats, anger, condemnation and control, create in their teenagers uncertainty, fear, powerlessness and loss of self-confidence.
3) Never label your teenager. Avoid at all costs labels such as *spoiled brat, greedy, miserable, ill-tempered, clumsy, arrogant, lazy, bad, childish* or *grumbler*. If his behaviour worries you, attack the behaviour, not the person. Also mention how you feel about the behaviour. For example: "I feel worried that you are unhappy and taking it out on your brother. What is wrong?" The labels tend to become sticky and very difficult to get off. Teenagers later become the label and it blinds them to their potential and worth.
4) Teenagers must feel that they are allowed to have an opinion without being condemned for it. Parents can encourage it by asking during conversations: "And how do you feel about it?"
5) Parents must listen when their teenagers talk. Listen with empathy, eye contact, a positive body language, do not interrupt, do not give advice (unless directly asked) and do not judge. This important element of communication makes teenagers feel that their parents care, understand them and appreciate them. This helps build their self-confidence.

3. SELF-CONTROL

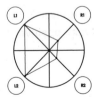

1) Parents must respect their teenagers' emotions, but must not allow them to have constant emotional outbursts – it is a mechanism to get attention, to force their will and to manipulate. If they get away with it, they start to enjoy the negative attention and later no longer react to positive attention at all.

PARENTS AND EMOTIONAL INTELLIGENCE

Parents' example in this regard is very valuable. By not being guilty of emotional outbursts themselves, they show their teenagers that there are other ways of dealing with problems. If, when they do have emotional outbursts, they apologize for them and admit their mistakes, they teach their teenagers an important lesson with regard to emotional intelligence.

Parents must also realize that such outbursts are often signs that other attempts from the teenager's side to communicate have failed. Therefore, while rejecting the outburst, (not the person) the parents must:
- immediately help the teenager to identify his emotions behind the outburst. ("Are you really furious with your brother, or are you disappointed about something that happened at school, or are you unhappy about something I did?")
- show understanding and empathy for the emotion. ("I fully understand that you can be so unhappy about it ... ")
- be honest about your own feelings. ("If you behave like that, I feel bad, confused, sad, but I also understand your feelings.")
- be available and willing to find a solution ("What will make you feel better?"). This is a very important factor in the development of emotional intelligence in your teenager. It shows communication, understanding, acceptance and respect for his opinion.

2) One of the major causes of loss of self-control in teenagers is parents who do not listen. Eye contact, positive body language, being nonjudgmental, showing signs of listening (nodding, "hmm", smile, etc.) are proof that I am listening.

3) The emotionally intelligent person is positive and focussed, also in difficult and stressful times. Here the parent must guide by his example. By constantly confirming their emotions ("I understand your disappointment, sadness, impatience ... ") the teenagers are brought on the same wavelength as the parents and imitate their behaviour in emotional situations. ("Mum is struggling at the moment, but she remains calm, she focusses on what she still has to do, she does not take it out on us – I can also do that!").

4. RELIABILITY AND RESPONSIBILITY

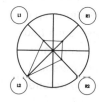

1) The teenager must understand that parents (and others) will trust him if he is reliable and behaves responsibly. This is emotional intelligence. Parents must naturally keep their side of the bargain, namely to show confidence in the teenager who has acted responsibly in the past. Parents should not expect adult responsibility in teenagers. The teenager must be home at ten o'clock in the evening if this is the agreement. On the other hand, he cannot be held responsible for the undisciplined behaviour of a younger sibling while their mum is out shopping.

2) Responsibility also implies that I admit my mistakes and do something about it. The responsibility of parents is to cultivate this climate in the home. The emotionally intelligent parent always apologizes sincerely when he has behaved wrongly or impatiently. He also takes responsibility for this behaviour, for example, "I am sorry I shouted

at you. I was irritated, impatient, angry. I know I should rather have ... " Never blame the teenager for this wrong behaviour – then he can do the same and refuse to accept responsibility for his behaviour.

B. SOCIAL SKILLS

1. EMPATHY

If parents guide teenagers and help them to identify their own emotions and if parents respect these emotions, the task of making their children sensitive towards the emotions and circumstances of others will become easier. Teenagers can be very self-centred – it is not unnatural. They are in the process of finding their own place in the world and discovering more and more about themselves. They undergo changes (physical and mental) and their appearance and what they are going to become one day, become extremely important. Parents must accept this as natural. However, teenagers must also cultivate sensitivity for other people's emotions and needs. Do not label your teenager as egoistic, unfeeling, etc. Rather use emotive language to make him understand other people's circumstances, for example, "It must be very lonely for Tanya if her classmates ignore her. Perhaps John acts like that because he feels rejected, shy or inferior; try to think how you would feel." Empathy also implies a responsibility towards others. Constantly ask your teenager, "What can you do to make him/her feel better?"

2. RELATIONSHIPS

The choice of friends is often a source of conflict between parents and their teenagers. Parents can exercise much more influence here if they adopt an emotionally intelligent rather than a condemning attitude. Do not insult, disparage or condemn your child's friend(s). Rather say how you feel about certain aspects of the relationship or certain behaviour. Say, "I feel worried because John uses such bad language. How do you feel about it?" rather than saying, "John has a bad influence on you. He swears and you are not allowed to associate with that class of person." Condemnation like this immediately makes teenagers feel that they have to defend the friend, even though they themselves condemn such behaviour.

PARENTS AND EMOTIONAL INTELLIGENCE 17

3. COMMUNICATION

1) We have already discussed how important it is for parents to listen to their children. Always be sensitive to your child's emotional signs and react or communicate sympathetically.
2) Regularly share information with your teenager, ask his advice and be receptive. Do not become angry or upset if he tells you things you would rather not hear. It is an important aspect of emotional intelligence also to listen to information and advice that is less pleasant and to be able to come to terms with it.
3) Communication must show integrity. Parents must not accept swearing, lies, gossip, insults etc. as part of communication. Your example as parent is very important here. Remember once again, do not attack, insult or label your child about such communication; attack the action or behaviour by expressing your own emotion about it. This is communication that children understand and can identify with.

4. DEALING WITH CONFLICT

We briefly repeat the steps for acquiring emotional intelligence (as in Book 1) as they also apply in dealing with conflict:
1) Accept that your teenager is allowed to have and show emotions. Do not try to convince him that he is not supposed to feel the way he does.
2) Help him to identify his emotions. Is he sad, angry, disappointed, ecstatic?
3) Be willing to listen before you act.
4) Help your teenager to further define conflict situations by linking them to emotions. "You are therefore disappointed in ... you felt insulted when ... "
5) Show constant signs that you listen and have empathy. Be patient.
Before you act or give advice, ask your teenager to suggest a possible solution, for example, "What will help you feel better about the situation?"
Eventually we must teach our teenagers that:
- conflict situations must be dealt with tactfully and sensitively;
- the conflict and accompanying emotions must be clearly identified;
- they themselves must think of creative solutions for the conflict;
- these solutions must be beneficial to both parties (win/win);
- openness and honesty must always apply.

CONCLUSION

You understand better now what emotional intelligence (EQ) is. Study the following table and identify gaps in your own and your teenager's emotional intelligence so that you can work at it.

SIGNS OF HIGH EQ	SIGNS OF LOW EQ
• expresses emotions clearly • not afraid to show emotions • not given to negative emotions • balances feeling with logic and reality • is independent and motivated • does not internalize disappointments • respects and is interested in others' feelings • not paralysed by fear and anxiety • understands non-verbal communication • takes responsibility for own emotions • uses emotions as aids to make decisions	• blames others for his emotions • cannot say, "I feel ... " • condemns others' feelings • is emotionally dishonest • exaggerates or belittles emotions • lets emotions build up and explode • no integrity or conscience • bears grudges and is unforgiving • is insensitive • is not available for emotional support • is uncertain, defensive and does not admit mistakes • is rigid and closed to new ideas • a poor listener • often feels bitter, inferior, the victim

"The time has come to concentrate on building emotional muscle and developing active emotional awareness, both in ourselves and in others."
— *Moira Katz* —

LEARNING AND STUDYING

> *"A balanced view between wholeness and specialisation is the key: the brain is designed to be whole, but at the same time we can and must learn to appreciate our brain's uniqueness and that of others."*
> — Ned Herrmann —

2 WHY DOES MY CHILD'S WAY OF LEARNING DIFFER FROM MINE?

How will I know how my child prefers to learn and to study and how can I help him do it better?

Parents must understand that the child will approach his learning and studying activities his own way and that every child in the house has his own preferences. One child will like history, while the other will hate it; one enjoys mathematics, the other languages or domestic science. It has everything to do with their **thinking preferences**. One wants silence while working at a neat desk, the other wants to lie on the bed with the book on the ground while the radio is playing loudly. Either of them will only enjoy his studies, the education that he receives, the atmosphere in the classroom and at home, as well as the type of projects that he must complete, to the extent that they agree with his brain preferences.

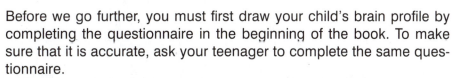

Before we go further, you must first draw your child's brain profile by completing the questionnaire in the beginning of the book. To make sure that it is accurate, ask your teenager to complete the same questionnaire.

Quite understandably the parent, when he wants to give the child advice and guidance, will do it according to his own personal brain preferences, just like the teacher teaches according to his own preferences. Parents and teachers must be well equipped in whole-brain teaching and studying so that they will know how to handle individual preferences.

Parents must also keep in mind that our school system has always been left-brain orientated and consequently right-brain thinkers usually come off second best. Because the child with left-brain preferences is catered for, a great number of pupils never reach their full potential, never experience studying as a joy, because their brain preferences are not in line with those of the parent, teacher or system.

The following is therefore of the greatest importance if we want to assist our children with their learning and studying. Place your child in one or more of the following thinking profiles and study the information well. Remember, a strong preference in a certain quadrant does not mean that a person will have equally strong preferences for all the thinking processes of that quadrant. Combination preferences can also be very complicated and their manifestation differ strongly from individual to individual.

Then study the hints that are given to facilitate learning and studying processes and especially to develop the weaker thinking preferences (p. 27). There are also hints for dealing with conflict areas between parents and children on this terrain (p. 33). The ideal would be for parents to discuss some of these suggestions with the child's teacher(s) and if all could co-operate to the advantage of everybody involved.

When you read the following, bear in mind what has already been discussed about the role of the parent in the future learning, studying and development process of the child in Book 1, *smart* PARENTS ... *children and teenagers*!

THINK AND DO: LEARNING AND STUDYING ACTIVITIES OF TEENAGERS

> *"I have offended God and mankind because my work didn't reach the quality it should have."*
>
> *— Leonardo da Vinci —*

Eleven profiles and a description of the principal learning activities represented by each, follow below. Select the one that corresponds to that of your child. We must remember that a high score in one or more quadrants does not necessarily mean that all the preferences of the particular quadrant(s) will apply and that combination preferences play a significant role. You know your child well and will be able to place him or her and know which "think and do" activities will apply.

THE L1 THINKER

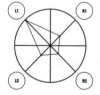

If his profile looks like this, he likes to:
- gather data and information, analyse and logically categorize it within a framework, but not to the finest detail;
- do research and delve deeper for meanings;
- listen to lectures that convey information;
- read non-fiction and handbooks about the subjects that he finds interesting (most school handbooks are written for L1 thinkers);
- study examples of problems and solutions and think ideas through;
- formulate a hypothesis and then test whether or not it is true;
- deal with knowledge in a scientific way;
- base his judgment on facts, criteria and logical argument;
- be precise and accurate in what he does. Therefore he is usually performance-driven;
- rather work with modern technology and hardware than with people;
- study technical and financial case studies;
- keep himself busy with the present rather than future possibilities. In a multi-cultural environment his interest will be roused by the technological development of the other groups.

THE L2 THINKER

If his profile looks like this, he likes to:
- work to instructions in preference to doing things his own way;
- keep to the proven way of doing things. He can therefore be reasonably conservative in his thinking;
- handle detail – is therefore not uncomfortable with a strong element of repetition. He accordingly acquires new skills through patient practising and much repetition;
- to listen to detailed lectures and take full notes;
- test theories and procedures, but not so much to prove that they are scientifically correct as to prove what is wrong with them;
- tackle his work and tasks step by step;
- receive programmed teaching and look for practical application of theories;
- plan well, draw up schedules and keep to a plan of action;
- give priority to the job at hand, because it is more important to him than the people who are involved;
- faithfully draw up a systematic report about the results of his projects;
- be a disciplined, dedicated, task-oriented person;
- draw up a budget and keep book of his expenses.

In a multi-cultural environment his interest will be roused by the procedures used and the organizational system that exists in the other cultures.

THE R2 THINKER

If his profile looks like this, he likes to:
- associate with people. Interaction will therefore be very important to him;
- gather information, primarily with the aim to exchange it and to communicate;
- look for personal significance in the knowledge that he gathers;
- listen readily to other people's ideas;
- learn by participating in group discussions;
- learn by teaching others;
- learn through sensory experiences – movement, touch, smell, taste, listen, look, test;
- play background music while studying (classical);
- make strong visual presentations;
- dramatize – the physical portrayal is important, not the imagination;
- use body language;
- show what he feels and experiences – cannot hide emotions. Therefore he often keeps a diary to write down his feelings and spiritual values;
- study person-oriented case studies and go on outings associated therewith;
- respect rights and opinions of other people, and the person will always be more important than the case. He likes to take care of and pamper people;

- have empathy with other persons. He does not like conflict and likes to build relationships of trust;
- become very enthusiastic about things – passionate!
  In a multi-cultural environment his interest will be roused by the interaction and communication with other groups.

THE R1 THINKER

If his profile looks like this, he tends to:
- look at things holistically and to want to know where this learning material or information fits into the broader picture;
- look for the total image and context of a new subject, not the detail;
- prefer lectures supported by strong visual presentation, as the visual plays a large role in his learning process;
- take the initiative and be actively involved in a variety of activities;
- like simulation exercises;
- ask "what if" questions and in this way generate many solutions to problems;
- play with ideas. He also often takes the lead in brainstorming sessions, where the wild ideas are more important than the team;
- develop hidden possibilities;
- not like a strongly structured, rigid environment;
- often appear restless, become bored easily and lapse into daydreaming;
- dislike routine and easily work with more than one project at the same time;
- think in terms of the future, notice trends, rely on intuition, not facts or logic. Therefore often tends to take risks and like case studies which are future directed;
- use ideas and information to produce something new;
- like trying a new way of doing, something just for fun.
  In a multi-cultural environment his interest will be roused by the multitude of ideas that other ways of thinking and doing will rouse in him.

THE L1-L2 THINKER

If his profile looks like this, he tends to:
- give preference to analytical thinking, factual reasoning and a rational approach, while he will also prefer the categorized, strongly organized, systematic and practical processes;
- require clear instructions and to want to know exactly what is expected of him;
- first collect information and plan in broad outline;
- thereafter draw up his action plan in more detail. It will be realistic and practical;
- execute his plan of action with dedication and to constantly evaluate and make changes. These will be practical and conservative rather than aimed at creating something new;
- be critical;

- want to work and study alone, or to operate in very small groups;
- be both performance and task-driven;
- not allow emotions and feelings to play an important role in his life.

THE L2-R2 THINKER

If his profile looks like this, he tends to:
- be very comfortable with the categorized, structured, systematic and practical processes;
- enjoy interaction with people, as well as handle learning contents emotionally, communicatively and personally;
- be practical and like doing things;
- plan very well;
- always want to involve people, like to work in a team and discuss his tasks or projects with other people;
- work in a safe, secure environment;
- usually take the lead with regard to organization;
- demonstrate; help, motivate;
- become enthusiastic about his work and projects;
- be both task and person-oriented.

THE R2-R1 THINKER

If his profile looks like this, he tends to:
- be person-oriented, empathic and sensitive;
- at the same time be very comfortable with generating new ideas and concepts, with diversity, experimenting and the quest for alternatives;
- before starting his work or a project, discuss it with somebody to get a broader perspective and test his ideas. It is important to him that his ideas and tasks are approved;
- want to know where the project or learning material will fit into the bigger picture, as he thinks holistically;
- expect that his instructions are given as challenges – not the mere repetition of previous learning material or tasks;
- comfortably generate many ideas;
- like teamwork and to motivate people;
- not complete things, because he is constantly busy with new ideas or with people and their problems;
- sometimes be very emotional and impulsive.

THE R1-L1 THINKER

If his profile looks like this, he tends to:
- think in terms of the future, try new ideas and ways of doing, like creative problem-solving and synthesis;
- at the same time think analytically, and have a rational, logical, objective approach to a task;
- get the big picture immediately;
- then, as a result of his analytical side, require clear instructions and will want to know exactly what is expected of him;
- analyse all the information and plan in broad outline;
- possibly have difficulty in getting on with it, as he repeatedly generates new ideas and methods;
- as a result of the combination of analysis and synthesis, produce new products and make his experiments come to something concrete;
- show entrepreneural qualities and think in terms of the future and determine trends;
- be very impulsive and take risks, but these inclinations will be tempered mostly by his analytical side.

THE 4 QUADRANT THINKER

If his profile looks like this, with the scores in all four quadrants nearly the same, he will tend to:
- not show strong preferences for the thinking processes of specific quadrants;
- have preferences in all quadrants – some will be stronger than others;
- have many interests so that he finds it difficult to concentrate on one task or particular field of study. His versatility can, therefore, be both an advantage and a disadvantage;
- sometimes be happy and motivated and other times unhappy and demotivated if he does not know what he wants to do;
- usually lack excitement and passion for a specific subject or field.

An example of an occupation in which such a person should be happy, is that of librarian. She can realize her preferences in the different quadrants in the information with which she works: factual, rational, logical, precise (L1); categorized, practical, systematic, explanatory (L2); emotional, person-oriented, spiritual, centred on values (R2); creative, innovative, experimental, futuristic (R1). Her daily task is analytical and focussed when she selects books and information for her wide range of clients (L1); it is very ordered and practised when she lends out books, receives them back, categorizes them and is engaged in the general administration of the library (L2); she works with people from all walks of life and must have empathy with their needs and problems (R2); and she must do exhibitions in an interesting, stimulating way and be open to ideas and suggestions (R1).

THE L1-R2 THINKER

If his profile looks like this, he tends to:
- love interaction and communication with regard to certain assignments and learning contents if he is a student;
- act intuitively and enthusiastically;
- usually know exactly what he expects of other people;
- research and analyse information which he discusses with other people and then proceeds with the task or project with other people or as a member of a team;
- be focussed, analytical, logical and rational, and be person-oriented at the same time;
- be critical, but at the same time display understanding and thoughtfulness;
- be both performance and person-oriented. Therefore he will usually succeed in motivating people and getting them to work enthusiastically. A good team leader.

Can you see that a financial consultant will have this profile?

Can you see that a sculptor will have the profile below?

THE L2-R1 THINKER

If his profile looks like this, he tends to:
- prefer the categorized, step by step, organized processes;
- have a holistic view;
- create new things;
- think in terms of the future as far as the content of his study course is concerned;
- think strategically and to plan as a result of his tendency to be future directed and his ability to notice trends, as well as his practical, systematic, structured preferences;
- constantly vary between new, exciting ideas and a conventional approach (for example shall I travel overseas after school and look for work, or shall I rather study and begin a career?); between impulsive decisions and their practical application; between taking risks and the need for security; between the repetitive practising of skills and the rejection of senseless routine;
- finalize things correctly because he is task-driven, but there are so many things he wants to start at the same time that he sometimes becomes very frustrated if there is not enough time for everything.

PARENTS CAN FACILITATE THE LEARNING PROCESS AND DEVELOP THE WEAKER PREFERENCES

"The secret of success is doing your ordinary work exceptionally well."
— John D. Rockefeller —

How can parents facilitate and develop learning and study activities?
Children are taught at school by teachers with certain brain preferences. They often do not receive education in their weaker quadrants. It can be that a right-brain child is taught history by a left-brain teacher. The teacher's presentation is analytical, factual, very structured, cold. The child needs a holistic, warm, emotional, informal, imaginative presentation and does not know how to study for or answer a "left brain" test paper. The following activities can help to:
- develop the weaker quadrants;
- further develop reasonably strong and strong quadrants.

Try one or two at a time, do not try too much too soon.
We are also going to give a mind map of one activity to help parents and children with the planning and holistic view of such an activity. **See how you can develop it further.**

L1 QUADRANT

Activity: Encourage your child to "play" the stock-market daily with some friends by consulting newspapers and other sources and reacting to them.

Other hints and activities:
- he must be able to study on his own in a neat and quiet place;
- information must be readily available – encyclopaedias, Internet, etc.;
- create opportunities for research and analysis of interviews;
- encourage use of summaries;
- practise his skills in logical argumentation;
- let him develop technical skills by repairing an old vacuum cleaner, or taking apart a broken computer;
- let him summarize a financial report and explain it;

- provide him with opportunities to work with modern technology, for example computers, new computer programmes, games;
- let him work out his study and sports programme for the next quarter;
- ask him to do a statistical analysis for the school newsletter of his school's sports results for the year;
- let him analyse South Africa's housing problem and components;
- encourage him to complete crossword puzzles;
- ask him to draw up a budget for the family;
- ask him to do research about cars, computers, etc. in a specific price class and then make a well-considered recommendation.

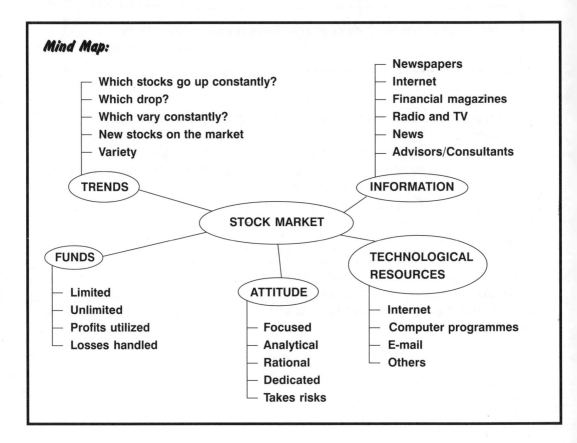

L2 QUADRANT

Activity: Practise your child's skills in planning

Other hints and activities:
- room and desk must be reasonably spacious and organized;
- he needs a space where he feels safe and secure when studying;
- there must be space for putting up programmes, lists, timetables;
- let him make notes;

- encourage him to apply theories in practice, for example chemistry experiments;
- encourage him to practise until he feels he has mastered the knowledge or skill;
- let him improve on a programme drawn up for an inter-schools sports day to make it run more smoothly and efficiently;
- ask him to compile a list of things to take on safari or a hike planned by his family or friends;
- ask him to plan a fund-raising campaign for charity and to help implement it;
- encourage him to build model aeroplanes (or any other models) by following the instructions step by step;
- let him draw up a budget for his sports or cultural society;
- pretend that burglars have stolen everything in his room. Let him draw up an inventory for the insurance company. He must indicate what it will cost to replace each item;
- let him draw up the categories of music to satisfy the musical taste of all pupils at the school fair's request programme;
- take any newspaper report and establish which four verbs are used most frequently;
- let him plan a class tour or family holiday to any popular destination and calculate the exact cost for each member.

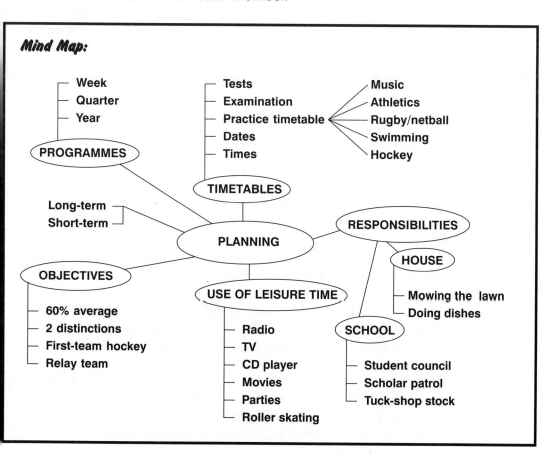

Mind Map:

R2 QUADRANT

Activity: Compile a list of things people do for you for which you seldom say thank you. Think of ways in which to show your appreciation.

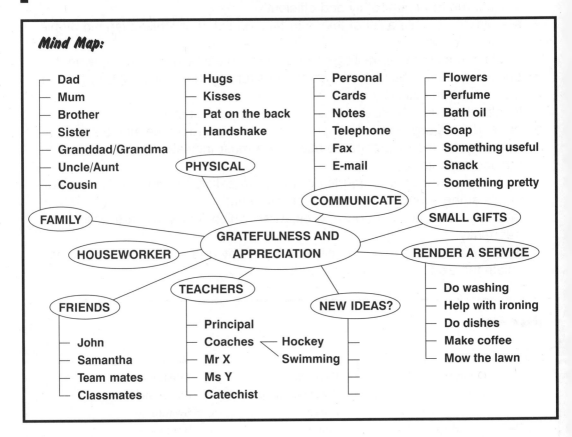

Other hints and activities:
- he wants to study where there is sufficient space to move about;
- allow him to have music in the background;
- he wants to feel comfortable, so let him lie across the bed if that is what he prefers;
- he wants to have his personal possessions around him and the notice boards and walls will probably be full of cards, notes and cuttings;
- allow him to study with a friend and discuss the work;
- allow him to demonstrate and dramatize to you the things he is studying;
- show understanding if study material affects him personally or emotionally;
- ask him to write a short note to a teacher or friend to say what he/she means to him (he does not have to send the note);
- encourage him to practise showing certain emotions, for example fear, anger, astonishment or joy in front of the mirror;
- let him write a note to his friends inviting them to a ball;
- ask him to get to know each child in his register class at school;

- encourage him to do things as a member of a team;
- get him to sit still for at least 10 minutes occasionally and feel emotional about something or someone;
- encourage him to listen for a short while to different kinds of music, including classical music and to try to enjoy and appreciate each piece. (See the section on music, p.44);
- ask him to read poems and try to find one that touches him emotionally. He must then discuss it with somebody.

R1 QUADRANT

Activity: encourage him to make creative posters or collages to decorate his room.

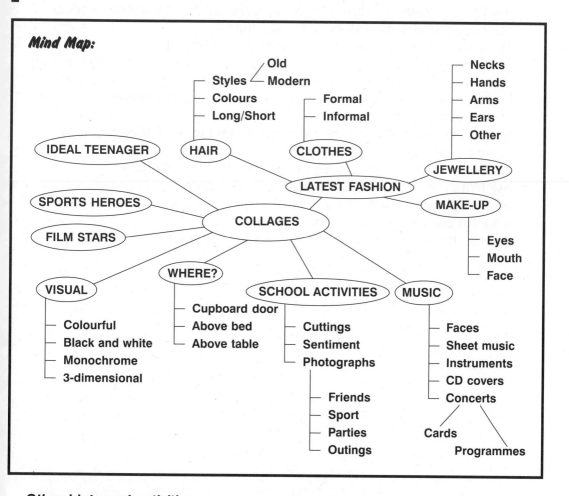

Other hints and activities:
- likes studying material with an artistic content;
- his notice board will probably display a lot of colourful and humoristic material;

- likes evocative and daring information and will buy magazines which may sometimes raise your eyebrows;
- wants to get a holistic overview of the learning material;
- will often make sketches and illustrations to concretise study material;
- encourage him to be innovative and to experiment;
- emphasize his uniqueness and allow him to do things his own way;
- enjoy and encourage his sense of humour;
- ask him to generate at least one "crazy" idea per day and put it on his wall or notice board. He can illustrate it if he gets a sudden fancy to do so;
- ask him to describe the craziest thing that he will do if he suddenly wins R100 000;
- ask him to close his eyes and imagine what his school, town or city will look like in ten years' time and then describe it;
- ask him to design a logo for an association or the family;
- ask him to create an original slogan to advertise any household product;
- ask him to read a short story and to illustrate it;
- ask him to design a new colour scheme for the house;
- encourage him to think of a new product that should be popular among teenagers and to design it. If he wants to market it, you must help him;
- let him design a T-shirt to promote his country as the venue for the next Olympic Games;
- let him ask some friends over for potjiekos (pot stew) that he made himself using his own, unique recipe;
- encourage him to make a sculpture out of wood, rock or clay;
- ask him to create a new dance style for teenagers;
- encourage him to write the words of a song that his favourite singer must sing. He can even compose the melody;
- ask him to liven up an uninteresting part of the garden.

DEAL WITH DIFFICULT SITUATIONS

> *"A torn jacket is soon mended, but hard words bruise the heart of a child."*
> *— Longfellow —*

There are a few things that can easily cause conflict between parents and children in the field of learning and studying. We are going to discuss three of these and give hints to the parent on how to approach issues of this nature in a whole-brain manner.

HOMEWORK

Homework is something that causes great discord and confrontation in many families. Parents in general think in terms of the future of their children and therefore want their children to perform well at school. For some teenagers this is not very important and they become irritated if their parents talk to them about homework, especially when they complain about homework that has not been done yet. Many children feel it is their own responsibility and they will do homework how, where and when it suits them and carry the consequences themselves.

Whole-brain approach
- explain to the child why, in the context of the 21st century, you think homework is important. It requires him to think analytically (L1) and strategically (R1);
- explain that you think he is mature enough now so that you can leave it to his own judgment to do it regularly and thoroughly. His thinking must therefore be critical (evaluating – L1);
- encourage him to draw up a timetable that provides for regular work times in his busy schedule (practical, systematic activity – L2);
- encourage him to stick to it, update it regularly and identity the problem areas (systematic, disciplined – L2);
- be interested and offer to give advice, to help, to help look for information, etc. (concerned, interested – R2), but make it clear that it will never be your responsibility and that you are not the one who must learn from it and grow (aimed towards the future – R1);
- allow him to study in the way that he prefers – lie, walk, play music, discuss with friends (acknowledge individualism – R1);
- arrange his room in the way he prefers it and do not criticize (empathic, accommodating – R2);

- praise him if he works hard and reward him with something to drink or eat occasionally (emotional, person-oriented – R2).

What other creative suggestions do you have?

HIGH EXPECTATIONS

Some parents place very high demands on their children to perform well academically. Sometimes it is because the parents themselves did not have all the opportunities, or because they never performed well themselves and want to experience it through their children. Sometimes it is because they themselves had performed well. Often the teenager just has the idea that his parents expect more of him and that they compare him to his brothers and sisters who perform well. Whatever the reason, it puts enormous pressure on him and the result is often tantrums and rebelliousness.

Whole-brain approach
- there are many psychologists and other specialists who can help you, by way of tests, to establish whether you are making unreasonable demands on your child (objectivity, realism – L1);
- explain that academic achievement is not the only way to survive in the 21st century and try to get him interested in practical things. Encourage him to practise these skills over and over until he has mastered them well (practical, disciplined, dedicated – L2);
- make him understand that participation and perseverence carry more weight with you than high marks, that task-orientation makes people reach their objectives. In the life outside everybody does not reach the top (task-oriented and purposeful – L2);
- explain to him that you do not expect more of him than he is capable of. Handle it carefully, so that he does not get the idea that you think he is not capable of getting very far in any case (understanding, warmth – R2);
- do not compare him with other members of the family who may perform well. Show that you respect and appreciate his particular talents. Teach him to compete with himself and not with others (empathy, respect – R2). As a family you are proud of the individuality of each member (R1);
- collect examples of people with relatively little intellectual talent (according to the old point of view) and limited opportunities who have reached great heights because they believed in themselves and were willing to tackle the future creatively (future perspective, entrepreneurship – R1);
- encourage them to produce many ideas and to experiment constantly (innovative, conceptual – R1);

DEAL WITH DIFFICULT SITUATIONS

- explain that tantrums only drain energy and make him a below-the-line person (unemotional, logical – L1).

What other creative suggestions do you have?

COGNITIVE DEVELOPMENT

Cognitive development is just as integral a part of growing into adulthood as physical development. It has to do with the teenager's becoming aware of his reasoning faculties and his quest for alternatives, using emotional intelligence, thinking patterns and intuition. That is the reason why he likes to reason and argue with parents and other adults. Parents often experience it as impudence, obstinacy and challenging of authority. Cognitive development also has to do with development of personality and identity. There is also an awakening of political, social, religious, cultural and personal values. The teenager often questions these values, rebels against them and regards it as his duty to solve the world's problems (at his parents' expense!).

Whole-brain approach
- expose him to as much information as possible concerning the issues that interest him. Show a lively interest in these matters and make sure that you are well informed about them. Reason comfortably with him about these issues without being pedantic and teach him to approach matters from different angles (focused, objective – L1; holistic, integration – R1);
- encourage him to participate in debates and discussions. He must naturally obtain the necessary information (L1) and practise his communication skills (R2);
- parents should see this cognitive development as a great opportunity to help develop the child's reasoning capacity. Play mental games with him (for example computer games, electronic 21st century games, Trivial Pursuit, brain teasers, chess) and encourage him to join, for example, a chess club (structured, strict compliance with rules – L2);
- cultivate the frankness in him to talk to you about controversial subjects such as abortion, teenage sex, capital punishment, racism (empathy, communication – R2);
- allow him to question the prevailing political, religious and social values, but he must suggest alternatives. Help him to develop his own value system (centred on values – R2);
- warn against closed thinking and emotional overreaction (creative, innovative, holistic – R1);
- cultivate in him a positive, creative attitude to life that is future orientated (R1);

- teach him creative problem-solving techniques (for example whole-brain mind mapping) and whole-brain decision-making procedures.

What other creative suggestions do you have?

CONCLUSION

For many children study has always been a less than pleasant and even bad experience, mainly because the teaching does not take their individual thinking preferences into consideration. For this reason they do not perform according to their potential.

Now that you as smart parents understand the whole-brain approach to learning and studying, you can play a very special role as facilitator and mentor. You can help the child to help himself and in this way discover and develop his various talents and intelligences. You can help him obtain a new certainty, seated in self-motivation, self-discipline and self-help. You can help him to realize that the key to change lies in his thinking – above-the-line thinking! You can help him to think in terms of solutions rather than problems and to set his sight on the future. You can restore his joy in and passion for learning that he had as toddler.

For this reason you as a parent must understand brain profiles, have an open, flexible approach, be accessible to the child, maintain an above-the-line outlook on life and apply whole-brain problem-solving and decision-making techniques. It will send your child into the 21st century with passion.

Good luck in this exciting challenge!

> *"Every word and deed of a parent is a fibre woven into the character of a child that ultimately determines how that child fits into the fabric of society."*
> *– D. Wilkerson –*

THE GENERATION GAP

"Adolescence is like a house on moving day – a temporary mess."
– Julius Warren –

THIS STRANGE CREATURE ... MY CHILD?

Did you experience the generation gap as a child and were you able to handle it then? Do you experience a generation gap with your children and other teenagers and can you handle it? Do not feel alone, there are thousands of us in the same boat – and there is hope for all of us!

In most families an estrangement occurs between parents and teenagers at some stage. It is as if the two groups attach value to and believe in different things, and each regards the other as being in the wrong. This is when the parent realizes that he is losing his influence on the child, whose friends' opinions now count more than his. This uncomfortable period is known as the "generation gap". It is a period that must be approached by parents in whole-brain fashion as the child is at his most vulnerable, during puberty and adolescence, and things can be done or said that can leave permanent scars on both parties.

During these development phases, it is not only their bodies which are changing, but also the way in which they think, feel, act and react. It will be good for us to think back to the period when we ourselves went through these phases.

1. PUBERTY

Puberty is the beginning of adolescence and sexual awakening when the body starts to change rapidly and strange feelings take possession of the child. With boys it is usually at around the age of 14 and with girls around 12, but it differs from individual to individual. With some the various forms of development start earlier and with others later. Children who develop late may become worried and anxious. Parents must ensure them that it will come and that some late starters even develop further than early beginners.

2. ADOLESCENCE

Adolescence is the transition phase between childhood and adulthood. It starts with physical changes and ends with the acceptance of the responsibilities of an adult in the particular society. These responsibilities lie in various fields, such as the social, economical, political and sexual.

For most teenagers and their families this is a traumatic period. The creative parent must regularly ask himself what he can do to make it as painless as possible. Therefore we must have understanding for the fact that the teenager must now, amongst others, develop and establish the following:
- his own identity
- control over his feelings, emotions and thoughts
- sexual preferences
- own value system and moral standards
- acceptance of the body and appearance
- acceptance of physical and mental talents
- satisfactory personal relationships
- long-term objectives and vision
- psychological and economical independence
- choice of fields of development and a career

It is normal for the teenager to experience fluctuating emotions very intensely during this period and consequently sometimes acts or reacts in a strange manner. There is confrontation with the parents and other members of the family; funny fashions; hairstyles and jewellery; peculiar friends; demands for more money and freedom; tantrums. The creative parent must then help him to distinguish between **acceptable** and **unacceptable** behaviour.

Many teenagers show little "deviating" behaviour during this period. This is also normal. However, the parent must not assume that there is physical growth only and no emotional or cognitive growth, with the concomitant inner confusion, and so leave the teenager on his own. The child constantly needs your attention and understanding, in spite of all indications to the contrary.

PARENTS, THEIR BRAIN PREFERENCES AND THE GENERATION GAP ...

> *When I ask you to listen to me and you begin to tell me why I shouldn't feel the way I'm feeling, you are trampling on my feelings.*
> – Anonymous –

The following discussion shows how various parents experience the generation gap from their respective dominant quadrants. Remember that these are only general indications and that everything under a particular heading will not necessarily apply to you. Look at your secondary and tertiary quadrants as well to gain a better understanding of your responses.

THE L1 PARENT

- You will probably follow a rational, logical approach to these emotional problems and may pass them off as "nonsense". The teenager may experience you as cold and unfeeling;
- you will feel that your authority is being challenged and will want to have the last word in arguments, or may even not tolerate arguments – "you do not talk back; you do not talk to me like that!"
- the lack of discipline that the teenager now shows with regard to his school work, duties in and around the house and his appearance, will go against the grain with you;
- you will feel that he must be more careful with his money and not spend it on any "junk" – referring to his music, shoes, jewellery and the like;
- you are performance-driven. If the child no longer performs well in sports (because he becomes more clumsy) and other fields, you will find it difficult to understand and will want to punish him for his "slack" attitude.

THE L2 PARENT

- Stability is important to you. Suddenly this obliging child is an unreasonable, moody little monster. You want to get him back to the old ways;
- your family's safety always comes first. Now you have a child who wants to

come and go as he pleases in these dangerous times and often even refuses to say where he is going. Stricter times and "grounding" him may be your answer;
- you just can't take his untidiness and lack of order any more. There is no routine, no study times or fixed bed-times;
- you are concerned about his lack of planning and his failure to work to a proper budget, leading to his "wasting" his money;
- you are task-oriented but it seems as if your child no longer wants to complete any task or assignment properly. He "can't get going", "sleeps all the time" and "will never be able to keep a job with that attitude";
- you believe in rules and regulations and they will be complied with "as long as I am the boss in this house!"

THE R2 PARENT

- If you are an emotionally mature parent, you will be able to handle your child well because you are flexible with regard to feelings. You understand the principle of give and take;
- you are sensitive to atmosphere, keep the channels of communication open and can negotiate;
- you have anticipated these problems and wait with clenched fists for the first minor confrontation. "He will know where he stands with me!";
- until last week you could still pamper him, give him a hug or a kiss, now he pushes you away and is aloof. What's more, he is always at the homes of his friends. You feel rejected, unappreciated ("Children aren't happy with nothing to ignore – and that's what parents were created for!" – Ogden Nash);
- if there is an argument or conflict, you become emotional, scream, scold, say hurtful things you do not mean, because you are hurt. Later on you have feelings of guilt while he goes on as usual and even ignores you. "Just wait until your dad/mum gets home ... ";
- you have taught your child so many good values, now he smokes, drinks, swears and you suspect him of ... You must take drastic steps;
- you become upset when he questions your religious and social values and starts going his own way;
- you try to understand the child, make allowances, make overtures, try to communicate, but he does not respond. It upsets you immensely. We often get the following response: "After everything I've done for you ... "

THE R1 PARENT

- You are often busy with so many things at the same time that you do not actually realize that the child is unhappy until he blames you for "not being there". Then you want to over compensate, which only irritates him more;

PARENTS, THEIR BRAIN PREFERENCES ...

- you cannot understand that you can no longer joke with him and act impulsively. He thinks you are "silly" and an embarrassment in front of his friends. Consequently you ignore him or become sarcastic;
- you show understanding for his individuality but suddenly he becomes ashamed of yours and you are criticized from head to toe – your figure, hair, shoes, make-up, eating habits, the way you laugh, the way you drive. It is enough to make one choke! You accuse him of egotism and being "too big for his boots";
- you are future directed and cannot accept that the child is not serious about it;
- you point out trends and possibilities that he can utilize, but he "wants to do his own thing". Then you wash your hands of him and withdraw your help and support;
- you become bored with this "psychological condition" and tend to belittle him.

 In the following chapters we discuss issues that cause the most problems and emphasize the generation gap. We give a mind map each time to show the holistic, whole-brain approach that parents must have. Study it and add to it, working with your teenager, if possible.

8 DEALING WITH CURFEWS

> *"... love them, feed them, discipline them and let them free. You may have a good relationship which will last a lifetime."*
> *– Mary G.L. Davis –*

Teenagers feel that they are becoming adults and should have more freedom. They often use the argument that their friends may come and go as they please and say only babies still need looking after. For the teenager, coming in late is the symbol of maturity and independence; for the parent it is the stronghold where they are still in control and can lay down the rules for the child's health and safety. Children often do not want to say where they are going, because they see their parents as nosy and "they won't approve anyway".

Whole-brain approach
- Discuss the question of times for going out and getting home with friends or other parents who have teenagers, also with his teachers and try to reach consensus about times that can apply school days, over weekends and during holidays. It is a good basis for your ground rules and negotiation (concrete information, realistic, objective – L1);
- try not to set fixed times, but ask what time he thinks he can be back and ask him to phone if he will be late. Let the times be open for negotiation (strategic, flexible – R1). When children have a say in this matter, they learn self-discipline and the chances are better that they will keep to the agreed times (L2);
- discuss the matter of transport: is there public transport? How safe is it, especially for girls? Must the parent fetch the child? Is it fair to expect the parent to stay up so late? (Safety, practical considerations – L2);
- "keep your cool" if you get unreasonable answers and say when you think he is unreasonable. Set an example of mature communication (R2);
- ask him to make the rules for other children in the house. Can his younger sister come and go just as freely? Where does the parent's responsibility end? (Realistic, critical, correct – L1; practical, regulated – L2);
- the important thing is that the child must know that his parent worries out of love for him (emotion, understanding, communication – R2).

DEALING WITH CURFEWS ... 43

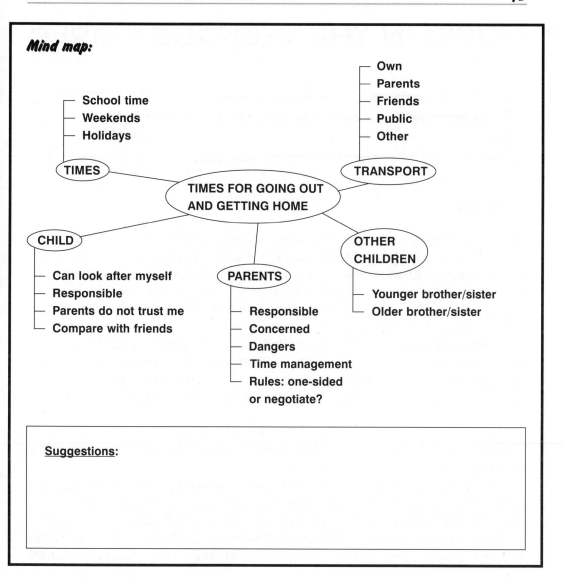

What other creative suggestions do you have?

MUSIC IN THE TEENAGE WORLD

> *"In everything there is music – for those who have an ear to hear."*
> – Lord Byron –

1. MUSIC

Music is a universal language that encompasses emotion, logic, mathematical correctness and language. Music has to do with frequencies, volume, rhythm, co-ordination, acoustics, melody and harmony. It is a bonding factor that tones down emotions, promotes unity and definitely has an influence on people's state of mind. Music is whole-brain, and therein lies the great value that we and our teenagers must discover.

These days parents know already that baroque music is good for children. As far back as 300 years before Christ, Plato referred to music as a powerful teaching aid. Nobody is ever too old to make music part of his life and its value can be rediscovered each day. All facets of the human condition are influenced by it.

The value of music for stimulating the brain must never be underestimated. It often forms the lost link in the whole-brain process and promotes the optimal development of the two hemispheres.

The wonder of music, and especially baroque music, is that we do not have to listen to it consciously, that it can also exercise its stimulating influence if played in the background. It can therefore be of great value if your child is studying, as it helps him use his full brain potential. Slow baroque music works in on the brain's alpha rhythms, making it most receptive for taking in information.

Associated with the working of the brain, there are different wavelengths that are situation and thought pattern related. Here is a short summary:

- *Delta waves:* Very slow waves, for example when you sleep without dreaming.
- *Theta waves:* When you are sleeping lightly and dreaming, usually just before you wake up.
- *Alpha waves:* The rhythm is not quicker than the heartbeat and is the ideal condition for learning to take place.
- *Beta waves:* Rapid waves such as when you participate in sport. It is like the rhythm of pop music and the music that is played in discos and at raves.
- *Gamma waves:* Occur during times of shock or trauma. Temporary loss of memory is sometimes experienced.

Therefore, when your teenager listens to baroque music, the alpha rhythms will become dominant, making him more peaceful and sharpening the memory process. The music only needs to be played softly in the background for it to have this effect. Loud, lively music will have the opposite effect and switch the brain to beta waves.

The central part of the brain is where emotion reigns unchallenged and where the urge for survival is seated. Skills such as logic and speech, on the other hand, have their origin in the cortex. When the child experiences tension and anxiety, the cortex no longer functions effectively. The central part of the brain takes over, the anxiety becomes a strong emotion pushing logic and calm reasoning out by the back door. Peaceful music can now help the child relax and guide the brain back to a condition of alpha rhythm, to promote learning and improve his attention span.

Parents often have to deal with a child who works hard and is able to recall and interpret the study material at home, but can remember nothing in the examination room. The harder he tries, the more anxious he becomes and the less he remembers. The reason is that the cortex has switched off automatically, making it impossible for him to look at the questions logically and put his long-term memory into operation. It is very important that the parent should create a peaceful climate at home before the examination and while the child is studying. Play baroque music at home and in the mornings before school or on the way to the examination room. Your child does not necessarily have to like this music, he will, in the long run, realize and experience its value.

Encourage your child to make music part of his life – not only by listening to it, but also by participating actively, for example by moving in time to it, dancing, playing an instrument, composing or singing.

Listen to different kinds of music with your child, from classical to modern pop music. Ask him each time how the specific type of music makes him feel. You can discuss your own feelings about it with him, without being pedantic or disparaging. You do not have to be an expert in the field of music, especially classical music. Just follow the steps hereunder to integrate music into your lives:

- Choose a composer from the baroque era, such as Mozart.
- Then choose a well-known composition, for example *Eine Kleine Nachtmuzik*.
- Listen to it repeatedly with your child until you both know it well.
- Choose another composition of the same composer and follow the same pattern.
- In this way you offer your teenager an opportunity to discover the wonderful world of music while improving both his memory and his listening skills.

Compositions that can be used:

BACH (baroque period)
Aria in G
Double violin concerto
Orchestral suites 2 and 3
Toccata and Fugue in D minor for organ

BEETHOVEN (classical period)
Overtures
Moonlight Sonata
Symphonies 5 and 6

BERLIOZ (romantic period)
"Symphonies Fantastique"

CHOPIN (late romantic period)
Piano concerto No 31

HANDEL (baroque period)
The Water Music Suite
The Messiah
Royal Firework Suite

HAYDN (classical period)
String quartet No 77 in C
Symphony No 88

MENDELSSOHN (early romantic period)
Symphony No 4
Violin concerto in E minor

SCHUBERT (early romantic)
Symphony No 8

SCHUMANN (early romantic)
Symphony No 1
Leider Lieder

VIVALDI
Four seasons

THE TEENAGER SURROUNDED BY COLOUR

> *"My eyes are made for light, for the green of spring, for the white of snow, for the grey of clouds and for the blue of sky ..."*
>
> *– Phil Bosmans –*

Colour plays an extremely important role in our lives, even though we are not always aware of it. Colour is like a state of mind: the colour you like in the morning may not be your first choice later in the day. This is important to remember if we have a teenager in the house. His kaleidoscope of emotions and the colour he favours, go hand in hand. It is not to drive his parents up the wall, but part of the wonder of his developing world. We must respect it and develop the potential and psychological implications of colour with him. All of us were created unique creatures and do not have to like the same things (and colours).

The teenager's individuality is now coming to the fore and you must allow him to decorate his room according to his own taste. It will also give you an opportunity to get to know and understand him better. He will often consult you in this, but never force your taste on him. See it as an opportunity to give him carte blanche for making decisions and responsibility within a safe environment. It is an important factor in his development into a mature person and you are letting him know that you respect him as an independent person.

Teenagers often choose red for their rooms. Red indicates intense energy and sexual development and is consequently a natural outcome of the development phase. Pink indicates love and security and you must address and support this need strongly. Boys will seldom choose pink, but will show their need for love and security in other ways.

Children who prefer a peaceful atmosphere, like blue, which counteracts tension and anxiety. Green indicates a need for space and privacy. Many parents become most upset when their children choose black. However, we must take into consideration that the teens is a period of great upheaval and discovery in the child's life. Black is a strong indication of individuality and somebody who has his own opinion about things. Your child wants to assert his individuality. Be sensitive in this regard and provide him with the forum within your family set-up to express his own opinions and realise his own identity. Encourage him to combine other colours with the black. The colour scheme can be striking and the other colours will break the feeling of isolation.

The psychological significance of colour
The impact of colour on our lives is subtle but powerful. Each colour has a hidden psychological meaning, for example:

- **Red**: A strong colour that is often associated with ambition. It also gives energy and counters negativity. If your child needs a boost, let him wear red.
- **Orange**: The colour of joy. Orange stimulates the mental processes and cheers up emotions. Give a dash of orange to counter depression.
- **Yellow**: Reminds one of sunshine. If your child is reserved and has difficulty in expressing his emotions, dress him in yellow and see the difference. Yellow strengthens your memory and helps you to think clearly.
- **Green**: Creates an atmosphere of peacefulness and makes one relax. It reduces stress and makes one feel calm.
- **Blue**: Promotes creativity and brings inspiration. If your child must perform a difficult task, let him wear blue to keep a level head.
- **Purple and violet**: Counter fear and set one's mind at ease.
- **White**: Creates a sense of peace and spaciousness. It also symbolises pureness and is morally inspiring.
- **Black**: Brings calm and is usually associated with quietness. This colour can also encourage ambition.
- **Brown**: Creates self-confidence and security. If your child feels uncertain, let him wear brown.

Play with colour, together with your child, and do not only brighten his environment, but also his state of mind and his awareness of colour.

Influence your child's appetite with colour:
Brightly coloured food and food that looks attractive, tastes better. Food is nature's way of providing energy, therefore, use food to support your child's busy, demanding life. Examples:

- **Red food**: Food with a red colour will provide energy and aid the immunity system. Foods in this category include tomatoes, cherries, apples, beetroot, red meat, liver and food made from animal products. Also food with a high iron content such as asparagus and green leafy vegetables.
- **Orange food**: Visually very attractive and stimulates the appetite. Oranges, mangoes, peaches, carrots, pumpkin, egg-yolk and pawpaws are good examples.
- **Yellow food**: Boosts the nerves and counters negativity. It is also good brain food and strengthens the intellect. Examples are nuts, butter, bananas, pears, pineapples and mealies.
- **Green food**: Forms the balance in the food colour spectrum, as it harmonises and offers resistance against disease. Grapes, figs, peas, celery, cabbage and lettuce fall in this category.
- **Blue food**: Is cool and has a calming effect. It can make your child peaceful

and help him to sleep better. Prunes, blueberries, black cherries, olives and raisins are examples.
- **Purple food**: Stimulates creativity and calms. Purple prunes, aubergines, thyme and purple cabbage have valuable colour nutritional value.

Experiment with colours and see what effect and value they hold for you and your child.

"Would the valleys were your streets, and the green paths your alleys ... "
– Kahlil Gibran –

11 TEENAGER PRIVACY

> *"Sanctuary is, in fact, a special strength. It gives more than refuge and release; it gives renewal. Essentially, sanctuary is a means of finding the power to face life on lifted wings."*
> – Margaret Blair Johnstone –

Teenagers start feeling the need for more physical and emotional privacy. They feel sensitive about their changing bodies and fluctuating emotions, consequently they want to be able to isolate themselves. This causes them to push their parents and other family members to one side, which often hurts and causes conflict. Small intrusions into their privacy may result in violent outbursts. Nobody is allowed in their rooms, they no longer want to share a room, they want to be alone in the bathroom, talk privately on the telephone or with a friend behind closed doors.

Whole-brain approach
- Show understanding for this need and point out your own need for privacy and personal space (individuality – R1);
- analyse the situation with your child and if there is not a separate room available for him, see where you can make a private space for him, for example a Wendy house in the garden (L1);
- allow him to decorate his room the way he wants to (individuality, risks – R1);
- have a modern name board made for his room with words like: "Do not disturb!", "_____ (his name) is master in this room!" or leave it to his own originality (innovating – R1);
- tolerate the junk on the floor, the open cupboard doors revealing bundles of clothes, the three pairs of jeans over the chair, the sexy pictures against the wall, the unmade bed, the smell of feet and dirty socks. However, undertake not to interfere provided he launches an "operation spring-cleaning" at least once a month and in the meantime does not leave his possessions lying about everywhere in the house (understanding, tolerance – R2; rules, order, consideration – L2);
- knock and wait for an answer before entering. Do not become angry if he does not want you to come in (emotional, understanding – R2);
- do not question him about his love and emotional life; wait until he wants to tell you himself. However, make him understand that you are always available if he needs an ear or some advice (R2);
- never read his letters or diaries, watch him secretly or eavesdrop on his telephone and other conversations. It can permanently damage the relationship

of trust (future-oriented – R1; understanding for feelings – R2).

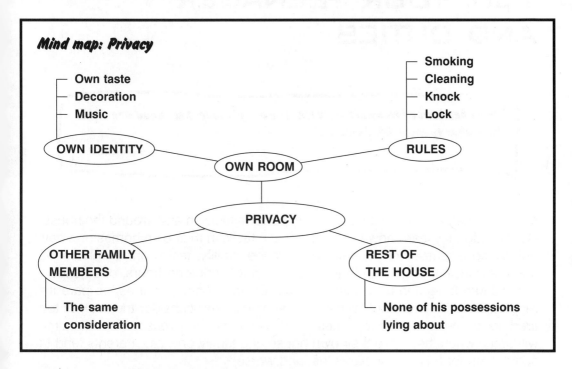

Mind map: Privacy

What other creative suggestions do you have?

12 YOU, YOUR TEENAGER AND DUTIES

> *"Who has learned to do his work without complaining, has found one of the best ways to make life bearable."*
> – Voltaire –

Most parents believe that children must perform tasks in and around the house. Not only do they learn how to perform these tasks in their own homes one day, but it also teaches them certain skills, responsibility, teamwork, involvement, and the principle of give and take. Parents who work long hours, often expect the children to lighten their task at home. Children often see it as the parent's responsibility. They are not "slaves" or "servants" and consider themselves too tired, for example, to do the dishes in the evenings. They reason that their time will come when they have their own house and family one day. Parents tend to scold them for being lazy, parasites, and worse.

Whole-brain approach
- Make a list of the tasks in and around the house with which you need help. Make your point of view on this issue very clear and allow the child to make a choice of the tasks that he feels up to (logical, rational – L1);
- help him to draw up his weekly programme and find times when he can perform these tasks (organized, practical – L2);
- show understanding for his tight schedule and help him now and then without making conditions. This will make him get the feeling of teamwork (R2);
- do not let him get away with slapdash work or neglect of duty and praise good work and conscientiousness (value system – L2);
- do not appeal to his feelings or play him off against his siblings or other children: "I wish you had your brother's backbone" (R2);
- do not bribe the child to do his share: "If you will mow the lawn on Saturday, I will buy you that ... " (values – R2);
- encourage him to think about the issue and produce time-saving suggestions or inventions. Reward his initiative (R1);
- think of a nice surprise now and then, like a family night out at your favourite restaurant to show your satisfaction with the teamwork (fun, innovating – R1).

YOU, YOUR TEENAGER AND DUTIES

Mind map: Duties in and around the house

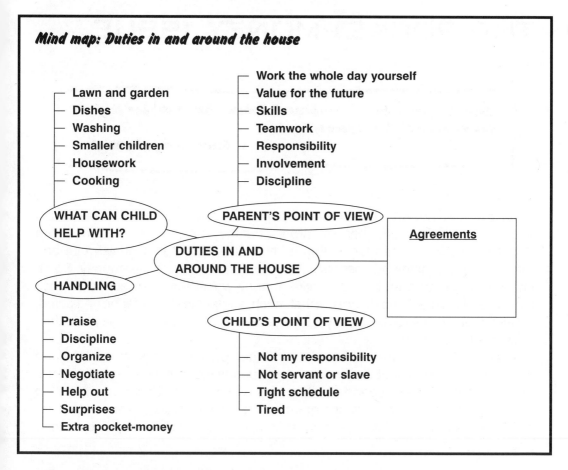

What other creative suggestions do you have?

13 THE POCKET-MONEY ISSUE

> *"Never tell people how to do things. Tell them what to do, and they will surprise you with their ingenuity."*
> — General George Patton Jr. —

To have his own pocket-money means independence to the child. He is becoming emotionally independent from his parents, but they still have this hold over him and it makes him dependent. What is more, the parent can punish him and force him to do things against his will by withholding his pocket-money. Some children get a large amount of pocket-money which they can spend as they please, and children who do not get that much, sometimes feel inferior, neglected, restricted and insulted, especially if they always have to ask for money and then receive a lecture to boot.

Parents often want their children to earn their pocket-money, or part of it and then have their say about the way the child spends the money, especially if he is not thrifty or a reckless spender in the eyes of the parent. Children experience this as a motion of no confidence or unnecessary interference. They hate to be compared with other children where managing their pocket-money is concerned.

Whole-brain approach

- Let the child make a list of his financial needs and discuss it with you. Listen closely to his needs. Negotiate the amount per week or month with him. Put your cards on the table with regard to your financial position if he expects too much (analysing, rational – L1; communication, understanding – R2);
- help the child to draw up a budget so as to prepare him for the future when he will manage larger sums of money (R1 and L2);
- allow him to spend his money as he wishes. Do not make any comments, but if he runs out of money, that's it (practical, rules – L2);
- as they become older and their social life expands, their needs increase. Many prefer to get more pocket-money and then pay for their own clothes, music, magazines, sweets, beverages and cigarettes, sports equipment, make-up, toiletries, gifts, movies and so forth. It can teach them to budget, they learn about the cost of things and the value of money (L2);
- offer to pay extra for special work such as washing the car, painting the roof, restoring furniture (L2);
- encourage him to earn some extra money by, for example, delivering newspapers, working in a business on Saturdays, or a restaurant as waiter, looking after people's gardens or pets or doing shopping for elderly people (L2);

THE POCKET-MONEY ISSUE

- praise these attempts and help now and then for the sake of the teamwork concept (R2);
- let him investigate interest rates on savings accounts and investments and see his money grow (L1);
- give advances if the child has overspent, but charge interest. It will teach him how to deal with credit in the future (R1);
- guard against cash and credit cards until he has proven that he can use money responsibly (logical, rational – L1);
- encourage entrepreneurship by word and deed (R1).

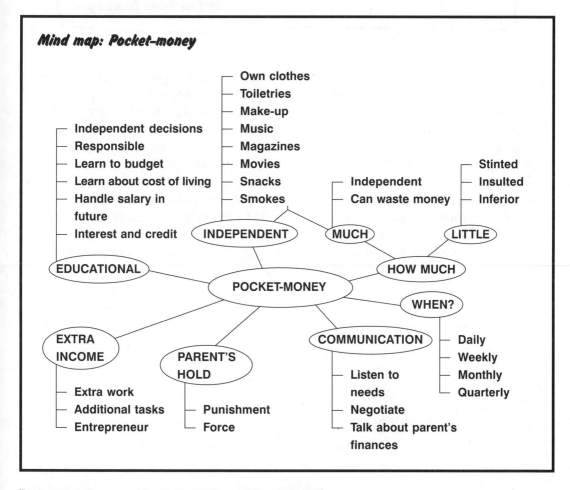

Mind map: Pocket-money

What other creative suggestions do you have?

14 THE TEENAGER AND EXPERIMENTING

> *"Life is a fragment, a moment between two eternities, influenced by all that has preceded and to influence all that follows."*
> – *William Ellery Channing* –

To experiment is a normal and healthy part of the process of growing up, provided that it is not overdone, and does not pose health or other hazards.

Teenagers often experiment with drugs, smoking, alcohol, sex, clothing, make-up, jewellery, tattoos, etc. This experimentation usually arises from the need to appear more mature and worldly-wise, to further his emerging freedom, to develop personal preferences, to be accepted by the group, to discover the excitement of risks and new theories and prevent boredom.

Parents are naturally concerned about the experiments, because they know, some from their own experience, that they do hold health and other risks for the children. They also know how freely dangerous substances are available and that they are usually tried where the parents are not present to see the effects.

THE TEENAGER AND EXPERIMENTING

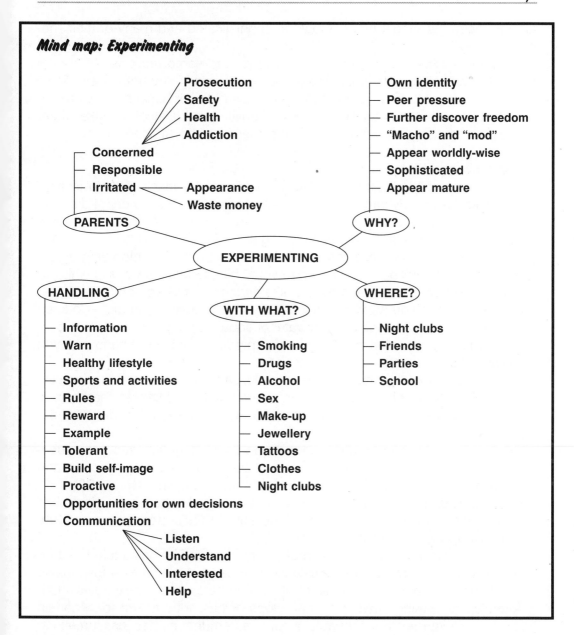

1. DRUGS, SMOKING AND ALCOHOL

Most teenagers do not use drugs, and those who do, usually use the "softer" types experimentally, but usually stop after a certain time. Most only use it at parties because it is then socially acceptable or the "mature" thing to do. Some teenagers will continue using stronger drugs and they are usually those with serious personal problems.

Children experiment with smoking, for mostly the same reasons as drugs. They see it as less harmful, their parents and other adults smoke everywhere around them, the media make it look so sophisticated and many of their "heroes" smoke.

Teenagers experiment with alcohol also for the same reasons. Alcohol is available everywhere and reasonably cheap. Especially at parties liquor flows freely. Many teenagers drive under the influence of liquor because they are too proud to admit that they are not capable of driving, or the alcohol makes them aggressive, so that they want to prove themselves to be "macho".

Whole-brain approach
- Inform your child about the availability, addictive influence, harmful consequences (physically, mentally and legally), as well as the variety of drugs in circulation. Do the same with smoking and liquor. Make a selection of reading and video material available (factual, logical approach – L1);
- discuss with him the occasions when he will be pressured into trying drugs, smoking and drinking. Try, along with your child, to think of ways in which to say no or to deal with peer pressure, like pretending that you become nauseous as soon as you want to use the product – "probably allergic" – to keep your glass filled by topping it with water or soda, keeping a lot of ice and constantly adding ice, always keeping an empty bottle of beer at hand as if you have just emptied it (safe, practical – L2);
- encourage a healthy lifestyle, for example participation in sports, debates, cultural societies, church associations, community projects, so that there is no time or place for drugs, smoking and alcohol (organized, disciplined – L2);
- undertake interesting family outings or do things together such as scuba-diving, hiking, trips in hot-air balloons and safaris where drugs, smoking and drinking just do not fit in (interaction, communication, teamwork – R2);
- if you smoke, stop. Explain why you want to stop this bad habit. Your child will be less inclined to start and will be able to resist peer pressure more effectively (logical, calculated – L1);
- advise your child never to start smoking, or to stop if he has started, but do not forbid it. It does not work. However, you can forbid him to smoke inside the house as it harms the health of other members of the family (rules – L2);
- promise something interesting if he stops or has not smoked for a certain time, like a journey, a reasonably expensive item that he desires, something that will make his friends jealous (innovating, alternatives – R1);
- set an example of how to handle alcohol. If alcohol is used in a family as a pleasant, normal part of social interaction, teenagers learn how to use it sensibly and safely (values – R2);
- teach him never to drink on an empty stomach. He can eat bread and butter or drink a glass of milk before going to a party and should constantly eat cocktail snacks or potato chips if he uses alcohol (practical, organized – L2);
- point out to him the serious danger of driving under the influence or getting into a vehicle driven by somebody who has had a lot to drink. They must rather phone you or take a taxi (safety – L2);

THE TEENAGER AND EXPERIMENTING

- win your child's trust and let him tell about his own or his friends' experiments. Never overreact or condemn. Share some of your own experiences at that age (communication, understanding – R2);
- constantly build his self-image and human dignity. If one feels good about yourself, you do not need "crutches" (R2);
- watch your child (but do not spy) and note certain signs that can indicate drug and alcohol abuse. Be proactive and immediately get professional help if there is reason for concern (future-oriented – R1).

What other creative suggestions do you have?

2. CLOTHING, MAKE-UP, JEWELLERY, TATTOOS

Teenagers feel the need to assert their own identity by means of their clothing, make-up and wearing jewellery and tattoos on different parts of the body. They will, as a matter of course, have to experiment to know eventually who and what they are. They often look strange, slovenly, mature before their time, even ridiculous, but acceptance by their peers is more important than their parents' opinion. They sometimes go to extremes just to provoke confrontation with the parent.

Whole-brain approach
- Show your appreciation for individuality and the development of an own style and personality. Accept him as he is and do not criticize his hair, clothes, taste and music (individuality – R1; understanding – R2);
- make him aware that you do not like it, but do not disparage him. "You look like a ghost with that green hair!" Rather say: "I liked the pink hairdo of last week better." (R2);
- do not forbid him to follow the teenage fashions and crazes. Be tolerant and show understanding for peer pressure. Point out the school rules where applicable, health risks, and let him spend his own money on it without criticism (R2 and L2);
- do not contemptuously refer to his clothing, tattoos and earring as "effeminate". Do not be sarcastic about make-up (Who gave you that shiner? Did some toddler mistake you for a colouring-book?) or jewellery (Here comes "jingle bells". Hullo! Look at this Christmas tree!) Try to say something positive (empathy – R2);
- look through fashion magazines together and discuss what is beautiful, practical, charming, chic, sexy or "cool". Show that you do have appreciation for modern things and can be a "mod" parent (alternatives, experimenting – R1). It teaches him appreciation for other people's tastes;

- do not judge your child or have doubts about his sense of values. Give him an opportunity to make his own decisions and prove value-judgement (R2).

CONCLUSION

Now that you have reflected on what happens to the child in his adolescence and why there is a generation gap, you should, as emotionally mature parent, be able to handle your child more comfortably. Even the most unemotional, disciplined child can have emotional outbursts and act strangely – sometimes contrary to his brain profile. Your knowledge of your own brain preferences and the whole-brain approach to difficult situations will enable you to guide him through this stressful stage without scars (to either of you). Then you can look back later on a wonderful, creative phase and enter the future along with your child, joyful and passionate, far above the line.

> *"There seems to be only one definite statement one can make about bringing up children – and that is that they should be accepted as individuals in their own right and their differences from their parents and each other tolerated and encouraged. Children develop most satisfactorily if they are loved for what they are, not for what anyone thinks they ought to be."*
> *– Anthony Storr –*

TEENAGER RELATIONSHIPS

5 RELATIONSHIPS WITH THE OPPOSITE SEX

> *"Our mother ... had grown up on a farm where families did everything together. How could I explain to her how much things have changed, that we kids scarcely admitted we had parents?"*
> *— Edmund White, A Boy's Own Story —*

In the chapter on the generation gap we referred to the changes and the accompanying emotional and behavioural revolution in the life of the teenager. It is also the time of separation between parents and teenagers and the building of new relationships with persons from the same as well as the opposite sex.

Parents sometimes feel that their children now forsake them and that they are only good enough to provide food, clothes and a place to sleep. They often do not approve of the persons with whom their children make friends and form relationships.

In their early teens children often have a close friendship with members of their own sex. Parents sometimes wonder whether they do not have homosexual tendencies. It is merely a transitional phase that they have to go through and parents must make them understand that it is normal. Mostly they start their sexual life by making friends with members of the opposite sex.

Sexual emotions and urges are caused by the production of hormones in the body. Teenagers must still acquire the skill to handle this aspect. They become intensely aware of the changes that take place in their bodies. They have sexual fantasies and are curious about sexual matters. These feelings often cause a form of anxiety and confusion. They have questions about love, sexual urges, sexual intercourse, whether sex is right or wrong, contraceptives, venereal diseases and pregnancy. They are also subjected to peer pressure to experiment with sex.

Girls are interested in close relationships with members of the opposite sex at an earlier age than boys. This stage of being in love, forming and breaking relationships, jealousy and day-dreaming, can be extremely disrupting and cause emotional disturbances. Teenagers often feel very sensitive and vulnerable and want to share their emotions with a friend rather than their parents.

Boys and girls also differ with regard to their reactions to their rapidly developing sexuality. With boys the sexual urge is more intense, with girls more romantic. Boys masturbate earlier and more frequently than girls. They also start experimenting with sex earlier. Both sexes fantasize a great deal, talk to their friends about sex and like flirting and petting. Boys like to boast about their achievements in this regard more than girls. Boys with "experience" are admired by their friends, so that those who have not yet had that kind of experience, are pressured into becoming a "man". Most sexual deeds are opportunistic, therefore not planned and can result in pregnancy. Involvement and guidance by the parent is therefore vital in helping children to develop healthy, satisfying and fulfilling interpersonal relationships.

THE PARENT AND HIS TEENAGER'S FRIENDS

Parents often believe that their child associates with the wrong person or group, or they have a problem with the person's social standing, hairstyle, clothing or habits. They may also be sensitive about the child's sexuality and be afraid that somebody may seduce him or her. Parents feel neglected because the child wants to spend so much time with friends, almost as if they are no longer good enough and home is just a hotel. When parents express their opinions about these matters, it is usually the proverbial fat in the fire.

Whole-brain approach
- Parents must understand that it is now very important for the teenager to belong somewhere, other than in his family. It is not that he wants to forfeit this support base – he merely needs an additional one. They have other things to talk about and personal matters and feelings to share. Acceptance by his peers means security to him and he will do nearly anything to display the group identity – hair, clothes, music! (Understanding, feelings, intuition – R2);
- show your child that you understand this additional need by encouraging friendships as a way of gaining knowledge of human nature (R2);
- do not belittle and gossip about his friends and their eccentricities ("That is a little monstrosity only a mother could love", or " I don't want to gossip, but ... "). Rather invite them to your home and get to know them better by showing genuine interest (understanding for individuality, quest for alternatives – R1);
- suggest a party at your house, but allow them to make the arrangements themselves (innovating – R1). Make it clear that what applies to the family, applies to visitors, for example, no smoking in bedrooms, no drugs or alcohol, (rules, safety, order – L2);
- discuss your objections (observations) openly with your child after giving the person you do not like a fair chance (analytical, factual, objective – L1; openness – R1);
- do introspection about the real reasons why you do not like the person. Might

RELATIONSHIPS WITH THE OPPOSITE SEX

it be a touch of snobbishness? Does, "No, really my child, he or she is not our class" sound familiar? (analysing, objective – L1);
- make it clear that you still trust your child's good judgement (R2);
- When there are cultural differences, help your child to understand and appreciate the other person's culture. See to it that there is sufficient information in the form of books and articles. Discuss television programmes about other cultures with your child and visit families of different cultures with him (L1 and R2).

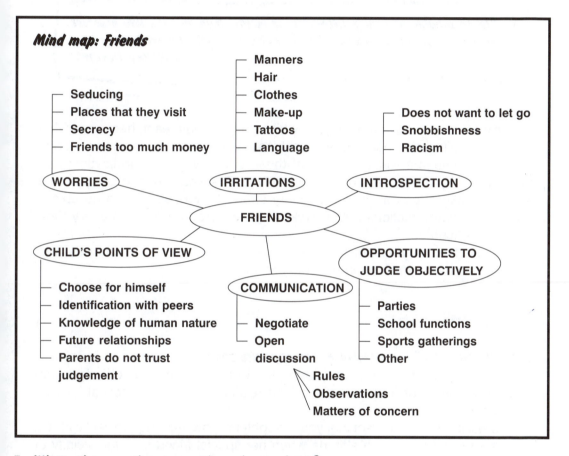

What other creative suggestions do you have?

> *"Of all things which provide to make life entirely happy, much the greatest is the possession of friendship."*
>
> *– Epicurus –*

16 PARENTS AND THEIR REACTION TO THESE RELATIONSHIPS

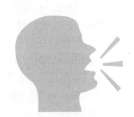

> *"To be capable of steady friendship or lasting love, are the two greatest proofs, not only of goodness of heart, but of strength of mind."*
> *— William Hazlitt —*

We next discuss the different ways in which parents may react, because of their dominant brain preferences, to relationships in which their children may become involved. Remember once again that these are only general indications and that everything will not necessarily apply to you. First find your primary quadrant, then also take a look at your secondary and tertiary quadrants to be able to understand your reactions better. **Tick off your normal reactions every time, where applicable.**

First we look at your possible reactions, and then how you can deal with them and certain situations in a whole-brain fashion.

THE L1 PARENT

a. Relationships with a member of the opposite sex
- You will probably constantly analyse and evaluate your child's behaviour for signs of a more serious love relationship or even sexual involvement;
- You will be quick to detect that your daughter is now wearing "sexier" clothes, has a more provocative attitude when her special friend is in the vicinity or spend more time on her appearance. You will also be quick to detect that your son who has always been a little slovenly in your eyes, now is more tidy when he visits his special girlfriend, uses aftershave lotions and deodorant, takes time to dress correctly and is becoming more modern. These signs make you suspicious;
- you may find that you have a desire to (and even do!) rummage through your child's drawers and read his personal letters and diary to look for signs of how serious or intimate the relationship is;
- you will probably make factual, rational reading material available to him about relationships and teenage sex;
- if you talk about the relationship, you may tend to warn him about emotional

PARENTS AND THEIR REACTION TO THESE RELATIONSHIPS 65

- involvement and how easy it is to reach a stage where you can no longer control your urges;
- if your teenager now starts to ask questions about sex and related issues, you may come to the conclusion that he wants to become or is already sexually active;
- you may tend to impose stricter times with regard to his comings and goings and to institute more rules than before;
- if your child breaks the rules and regulations, no matter how insignificant, you will tend to become introspective about where you have failed as parent.

b. Relationships with a member(s) of the same sex
- Boys and girls usually have one or more very good friends in their teens with whom they share their most intimate feelings. They also spend a great deal of time together, often just the two of them, sleep over on weekends and will defend each other at the smallest sign of criticism or problems. As L1 parent you may tend to be sceptical sometimes about this intense friendship and look out for signs of homosexuality;
- you may tend to take note of the social standing of your child's friend or girlfriend and that particular family's status in society. You will probably also want to know and approve the family history;
- you may even tend to watch the friend closely and analyse his habits and manners in order to establish whether he is the right friend for your child. You will carefully note what he can talk about and like it if he is well informed on a variety of subjects. "Empty heads" are out!

c. Relationships with other individuals and groups
- You will probably tend to analyse your child's relationship with other individuals and groups, for example an older person, a teacher, coach, social group, sports friends and church groups in order to determine whether there are any bad influences;
- you will analyse your child's behaviour towards these individuals and groups and make sure that he can hold his own and is not wronged or exploited;
- when you talk to your child about these individuals or groups, you will probably have a logical, rational approach and point out the advantages and disadvantages that the relationship holds for the child. You may use expressions like: "X is too old/young for you ... Too much of a good thing ... You are wasting your time ... Get your priorities in order ... ";
- where school and other weekend or holiday camps and school tours are concerned, you may want to know exactly who are going and how they will be supervised. You may tend to refuse to let your child go if there is somebody who, in your opinion, is undesirable. You will probably prefer study or educational camps to camps of a more social nature and not like mixed (boys and girls) tours very much.

THE L2 PARENT

a. Relationships with a member of the opposite sex
- You may tend to watch your son or daughter systematically for signs of a special relationship to determine how far the relationship has progressed and whether your child is "safe". You may even involve other members of the family in this;
- you will also watch your child constantly for signs of change with regard to clothing, make-up, neatness, untimely visits and telephone calls. You will want to deduce from this how deep the involvement with the special friend or girlfriend goes;
- You may also want to (and even do) rummage through your child's personal possessions, read his letters, eavesdrop on telephone calls, just to make sure he is safe and on the right track with the relationship;
- you will probably make factual reading material available to your child about "what every child should know", especially reading material with a systematic, practical approach;
- if you talk about the relationship, you will tend to talk about the stable, unemotional and safe aspects;
- if your teenager now starts to ask questions about sex and related issues, you may think that he is preparing himself for sexual activities, or that he is already involved. It may upset you;
- you may now tend to make your child follow a stricter routine – set times for homework, sport, household duties, church activities. You want them to spend less time alone together and force other activities on them. You will prefer them to become more involved in group activities;
- if your child does break certain rules and regulations, you will analyse the process of upbringing step by step to find out where you have failed as a parent.

b. Relationships with a member(s) of the same sex
- Boys and girls usually have one or more very good friends in their teens with whom they share their most intimate feelings. They also spend a great deal of time together, often just the two of them, sleep over on weekends and will defend each other at the smallest sign of criticism or problems. As L2 parent you may tend to be sceptical sometimes about this intense friendship and to look out for signs of homosexuality;
- acceptance of the person in your family circle will be important to you. The child will have to be able to fit in. You will probably make an effort to find out more about his family and their mutual relationships, as well as their prosperity, social standing and the circles in which they are moving;
- you will watch the child's clothing, taste, habits and manners in order to establish whether he is the right friend for your child. You will take note of his use of language and what he can talk about. You will probably immediately like him or her if he or she is helpful, practical, neat and reasonably conservative. Slovenliness, strange clothing and tattoos are out!

c. Relationships with other individuals and groups

- You will probably keep an eye on your child's relationships with other individuals and groups, for example an older person, a teacher, coach, social group, sports friends and church group. You will want to establish whether there may be any bad influences. Your child and family always come first;
- you will therefore watch your child's behaviour towards these persons and groups to make sure that he can hold his own and is not wronged or exploited. He must be safe in that company;
- when you talk to your child about these individuals or groups, you will probably follow a practical, rule-bound, safe approach. You may use phrases such as: "I do not want you to be disappointed or hurt ... Look out, you are going to burn your fingers ... I know trouble when I see it ... Once a good-for-nothing, always a good-for-nothing."
- where school and other weekend or holiday camps and tours are concerned, you will immediately want to know who are going, how they will be supervised and how they will travel. You will even offer to go along or to drive the child just to check out the situation. You will probably prefer camps where practical, physical work will be done and where there is not much time for courting.

THE R2 PARENT

a. Relationships with a member of the opposite sex

- You will probably adopt an empathetic attitude when your child shows signs of a special relationship and try to enter into the spirit of it;
- you may tend to encourage relationships, especially if you like your child's friend or girlfriend, and will try to understand and even condone signs of dressing "sexy", provocative attitude, sudden neatness and modernity;
- you probably won't rummage through your child's personal possessions or read his letters, but rather hint and ask interested questions to find out how serious or intimate the relationship is;
- you will probably look for and make available to your child reading matter with a beautiful, empathetic attitude to the adolescent and his love life and a value system approach to teenage sex;
- if you talk about the relationship, you may tend to convey to your child that you understand the emotion, experienced it yourself and will be there for support and advice. You will address the problem of storm and stress and warn against it;
- if your teenager now starts to ask questions about sex and related issues, you will wonder how involved he already is in a sexual relationship and hope he will confide in you;
- you may consider setting stricter times for going out and getting home and be more prescriptive, but you keep on hoping that the child's good judgement and the values you taught him will prevail so that you will not need to institute drastic measures;

- if your child does break certain rules and regulations, you may react very emotionally, scream and scold, and lie awake nights thinking that you have failed as a parent, in spite of your good intentions.

b. Relationships with a member(s) of the same sex
- Boys and girls usually have one or more very good friends in their teens with whom they share their most intimate feelings. They also spend a great deal of time together, often just the two of them, sleep over on weekends and will defend each other at the smallest sign of criticism or problems. As R2 parent you may tend to be jealous of this intense friendship and even try to become part of it. You will probably not think of homosexuality, but rather remember that you yourself at that stage had such close relationships;
- you will probably want to get to know your child's friend or girlfriend better and evaluate him or her as a person, rather than determine his or her social standing and the family's status in society;
- you may tend to try to spend time with your child's friend in order to get to know more about him from his habits, manners and conversation. In this way you will decide whether he is the right friend for your child. You will note things like thoughtfulness, respect for people, good communication and whether he behaves decently towards your child. An unfeeling, thoughtless, crude person is out!

c. Relationships with other individuals and groups
- You will want to be informed about your child's relationships with other individuals and groups, for example an older person, a teacher, coach, social group, sports friends and church group so that you can see whether there are any bad influences;
- you will therefore also want to observe your child's behaviour towards these individuals and groups to see whether he can hold his own, and especially if he applies the principles you have taught him; whether he is wronged or exploited; whether you might not be able to fulfil the role of the particular group or individual yourself;
- when you talk to your child about these individuals or groups, you will probably have an accommodating, understanding approach but spell out your concern about things that bother you. You may use phrases such as: "I don't really have something against X, but I just wonder ... They look like nice children to me, but aren't they too ... ? Son, what do you and Mr Y talk about when you are alone? What nonsense is this ... ";
- where school and other weekend or holiday camps and school tours are concerned, you will immediately want to know what the programme is and who will present it. You will probably like the idea of interaction with a variety of children, but will want to make sure that values and principles are maintained. You prefer participation in a group rather than that the children spend time together in pairs.

PARENTS AND THEIR REACTION TO THESE RELATIONSHIPS

THE R1 PARENT

a. *Relationships with a member of the opposite sex*
- You will probably look holistically at your child and his special friend or girlfriend and their involvement in the relationship and intuitively determine how serious it is and whether they are sexually involved;
- you will detect quickly that your daughter now dresses "sexier", becomes more provocative; spends more time on her appearance; that your son has become tidier, uses after shave and deodorants, has become more modern or reveals other behavioural changes. These signs will not so much make you suspicious as interest you, so that you will be on the lookout to see where it will lead;
- if you find your child's personal letters or diary (you will probably not look for it, except if you do it for fun), you will be in two minds about whether to read it or not. You will like to confirm your suspicions about the relationship;
- you will look for reading material that addresses teenager relationships and sex in an interesting, imaginative and modern way and give it to your child;
- if you talk about the relationship, you may tend to approach it holistically and make the child understand where it fits into his or her life, priorities, the advantages and disadvantages of a serious relationship at that stage, the dangers, perspective of the future, etc;
- if your teenager now starts asking questions about sex and related issues, you may come to the conclusion that he wants to experiment or may already be sexually active. You will now recommend these books and recommend contraceptives;
- you may consider stricter rules, as well as other restrictions, but will negotiate with the child and try not to be too rigid;
- if your child does break the rules and regulations, you will tend to see it from a broader perspective – it is not the end of the world. You will take his individuality into consideration, as well as your own and try to establish what you as parent did that made the child react like that.

b. *Relationships with a member(s) of the same sex*
- Boys and girls usually have one or more very good friends in their teens with whom they share their most intimate feelings. They also spend a great deal of time together, often just the two of them, sleep over on weekends and will defend each other at the smallest sign of criticism or problems. As R1 parent you may find this intense relationship interesting and intuitively know whether or not there are homosexual tendencies;
- you will approach the special friend as a total person to see whether he is the right friend for your child. You will look at his habits and manners, his use of language, clothes and neatness (modernity will not bother you), whether he can talk about interesting things, his sense of humour, his plans for the future. Dull, unimaginative persons are out!
- the friend's social standing and his family's social status will probably not be

very important to you, provided that he is an interesting individual who can enrich your child's life in various ways.

c. Relationships with other individuals and groups
- You will probably look at your child's relationships with other individuals and groups, for example an older person, a teacher, coach, social group, sports friends and church group to determine what good and bad influences are present. You have an intuitive feeling for it;
- you will also watch your child's behaviour towards these individuals and groups to see whether he can hold his own and deal with the influences. You will probably encourage him to become involved in a variety of relationships in order to gain knowledge of human nature;
- when you talk to your child about these individuals or groups, you will have an open approach and point out the wide range of things that one can learn from them and the fun one can have. You may use phrases such as: "X is not actually the most exciting ... It should be a wonderful opportunity ... Do you see a future in that? Don't be obsessed with one little thing ... ";
- where school and other weekend or holiday camps and school tours are concerned, you will probably want to know where they are going and what the programme will be. You will want to know whether it will be an interesting learning experience for your child and what he will gain from it, even if it is only a lot of fun. You believe he will behave himself, because you have taught him everything.

17 OTHER RELATIONSHIPS

> *"We attract hearts to the qualities we display; we retain them by the qualities we possess."*
>
> — Scad —

As we have often said, one's brain dominances determine one's behaviour and actions. Therefore, we can expect that our behaviour towards our teenager, as well as the person or persons with whom he or she is in a relationship, will have a direct link with our thinking preferences. Just as we as adults have to try to adopt a whole-brain approach at all times, such as when we have to make important decisions, take over leadership, plan strategy or communicate about something important, we must also attempt to approach our children's relationships in whole-brain fashion. When we follow our dominant brain preferences, we may act and react unilaterally and sometimes say or do things that leave scars or cause further damage.

We want to emphasize once again that a mind map is a wonderful, creative way in which to look at a situation in whole-brain fashion. When you want to look at your child's relationships with other people and even the parents and family, draw up a mind map and act according to the perspective that it provides.

We will also discuss how you can handle the above and other reactions to your child's various relationships in whole-brain fashion. Read again what has been discussed in Chapter 6 with regard to the whole-brain handling of certain problem situations with teenagers.

1. RELATIONSHIPS WITH A MEMBER OF THE OPPOSITE SEX

1. **You suspect that your child may become serious about the relationship or is sexually involved.**
   - Do not act rashly or confront the child immediately. Analyse the situation (L1); confirm your facts (L2); try to have a talk with your child about the matter at the right time and show that you understand his feelings (R2); try to give the child a broader perspective about the matter (R1).
   - Develop a relationship of trust so that the child has the frankness to talk to you (R2).
2. **You observe that your child is acting differently – she wears "sexier" clothes, has a provocative attitude, spends more time on her appearance, or your son is suddenly tidier, uses after shave and deodorants and dresses more modern.**

- Do not show that you are becoming suspicious, or even tease the child, rather compliment him (L2, R1).
- Invite the friend or girlfriend home and observe how they act towards each other (L1). Objectively discuss with them both, together or individually, things that are bothering you, without condemning (R2). Give them a chance to give their side of the story (L2) and show that you have an open mind (R1).
- However, make your rules clear (L1). Both must be convinced that your action is motivated through love and because you care about both of them (R2).

3. You would like to find out how serious and intimate the relationship is.
   - Take into consideration what has already been discussed in point one above. Do not rummage through your child's cupboards and drawers for signs that can confirm your suspicions. Also do not read his personal letters and diary without his permission. If he finds out, it can permanently damage the relationship of trust, especially at his emotional, uncertain stage (L1, R2, R1).
   - Rather win his trust so that he wants to share his secrets with you because he trusts your good judgement – you won't laugh, tease, become angry or condemn, only understand! (L2, R2).

4. You feel you should provide him with information about relationships and teenager sex.
   - When you put books, magazine articles and other material at your child's disposal, remember that you want a whole-brain approach.
   - Remember further that informative material can never replace a parent's duty with regard to sex education and how to deal with relationships. It must only serve as additional information and starting points for discussions (R1).
   - If we take into consideration that most children get their "sex education" from school friends, older children, movies, videos, letters in magazines, magazine articles and even pornography, the parent's role as reliable expert is once again emphasized (L1, R2).
   - Therefore, make sure that the material which you provide:
     ~ contains the correct facts (L1);
     ~ provides what the child needs at that stage (especially younger children), not less (L1);
     ~ follows a step-by-step practical approach (L2);
     ~ takes into account the child's various and changeable emotions, uncertainties, problems and sensitivities (R2);
     ~ is visual and explicit, though in good taste and is presented with the necessary respect and creativity (R1);
     ~ talks at the child's level – not down to him – and in his language (L1, L2, R2).

5. If your teenager starts asking questions about sex and related issues, you may deduce that he wants to become, or is already, sexually active.
   - Do not ask him pertinently or confront him, rather encourage a conversation (R1).
   - Use opportunities such as episodes in movies or videos, matters that are addressed in programmes (for example Oprah Winfrey), letters of teenagers in magazines, to ask the child's opinion on issues such as pre-marital sex, abortion, venereal diseases, living together, contraceptives, assault, sexual harassment, masturbation and so on (R1, R2, L2).

OTHER RELATIONSHIPS

- Many parents immediately switch off the TV or radio, forbid children to watch the movie further or tear sex articles from magazines. It breaks down communication between you and his trust in you (L2, R2).
- Discuss the source, the presentation, the quality of the arguments analytically and objectively (L1).
- Be willing and prepared to state clearly your point of view about each subject, not to condemn or belittle his point of view, but to reason about it and advise with understanding (L1, L2, R2).
- Explain on which value system you base your point of view and ask about his (R2).

6. When you are talking about his specific relationship:
   - Do not become personal about the appearance, taste, habits or use of language of the friend or girlfriend. Do not express any destructive criticism; try saying something positive (R2, R1).
   - Express your personal opinion unemotionally and objectively (L1).
   - Do not disparage your child's behaviour ("cheap", "tart", "flirt") rather ask the reason for it (R2, L2).
   - Do not immediately warn against what may happen or will happen. Test the child's judgement by asking what he or she will do if the following situations arise (L2), for example, he or she:
     ~ "gets fresh" while you two are alone at home
     ~ starts undressing and invites you to become more "comfortable" too
     ~ suggests that you watch a porn video
     ~ says that you must prove your love by means of sex
     ~ says that if you have not "done it yet" you know nothing about life and your friends will laugh at you
     ~ suggests that you use alcohol or drugs
     ~ suggests that you spend a night or weekend together
   - discuss the situations openly, give advice and do not forget your sense of humour (R1, R2, L2).

7. You may now think of stricter rules and regulations about times for going out and getting home, opportunities for being together and the way they dress.
   - Do not overreact and make unrealistic regulations. Judge each case on its merit and negotiate with your child and his or her friend about times and events that suit everybody (L1, L2, R1).
   - Make it clear what your house rules are, such as no "clinging", no caressing in front of other members of the family, no visiting in the bedroom or switching off the light (L1, L2).
   - Do not forbid the children to do things, such as wearing certain clothes, swimming together at night, calling each other, going to dances, having a drink, smoking, or doing drugs. Do not, on the other hand, force them to do things such as visiting a grandparent with the family just in order to keep them apart. Make your point firmly and make it clear that you rely on their good judgement and that you trust them unconditionally (L2, R2).
   - Also read what we have already said about this in Chapter 1.

8. If your child does break the rules and regulations, do you feel that you have failed as a parent?
   - Do not condemn yourself, become stressed or feel depressed. Have a calm conversation with your child and explain that you are disappointed because you have trusted him or her and that the trust has been temporarily betrayed (L1, R2).
   - Emphasize once again that your rules are there to protect and support him or her, not to restrict or wrong them (L2, R2).
   - Make your child understand that it is not the end of the world, that all of us make mistakes, that you also broke rules as a child and that you will still trust him or her in future (R1, L2). Do it!
   - First listen to the child's reason why he or she broke the rules and avoid an emotional outburst (L1).

Mind map

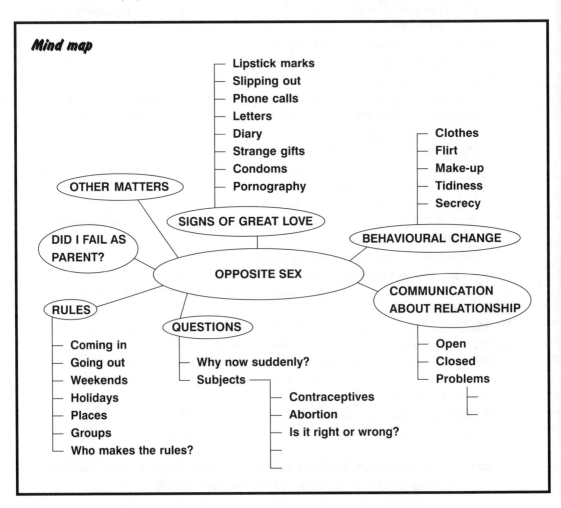

OTHER RELATIONSHIPS

2. RELATIONSHIPS WITH MEMBER(S) OF THE SAME SEX

1. Teenagers usually have one or more very good friends of the same sex with whom they share their most intimate feelings. They also spend a great deal of time together, often very privately, sleep over on weekends and will defend each other at the smallest sign of criticism or problems.
   - Do not be sceptical or even jealous and feel excluded when this happens. It is very natural and almost every teenager experiences it. Refrain from being sarcastic and perhaps referring to "gays" (R2).
   - Do not watch the situation overtly or even ask questions that may make the child think that you doubt his sexual orientation. Rather talk to him about his friend(s) and what the friendship means to him. Talk about your own friends and the value of sincere friendship (R1, R2).
   - Do not try to eavesdrop on their conversations to find out how intimate the relationship is, forbid them to sleep or take a bath together. You may wake up sleeping dogs (L2, R2).
   - Rather invite the friends home and show that you appreciate the friendship. Be a parent to talk to, share things and have fun with (L2, R1). They can sometimes become part of the family to everybody's advantage and happiness.
2. The social standing of your child's friends:
   - Few things make children as rebellious as when their parents are snobbish and regard their friends as "not their class". Guard against asking questions and saying things that can leave this perception with children (L2).
   - Set an example for your child of a person who looks at values and qualities rather than money, status and social prestige (R2, R1).
   - Show your child that you understand peer pressure and respect group identity (R2, R1).
3. Is he or she the right friend for my child?
   - Do not openly watch or analyse the friend's habits and manners so that your child gets the idea that you are evaluating him as a suitable person to associate with. Rather show that you like him until you are proved wrong (L1, R1).
   - Do not purposely test his ability to talk about certain subjects (especially those that interest you), try to test his general knowledge or how informed he is about certain matters. It will irritate your child immensely and cause them to avoid your company. Rather try to join in their conversation if they allow you to, but do not be pedantic or arrogant (L2, R2).
   - Do not purposely test his values and principles and let your child become aware that you want to determine whether the friend will be a good or bad influence. He will not have much respect for your tact and integrity. Base your judgement on natural interaction and communication (L2, L1, R2).

Mind map

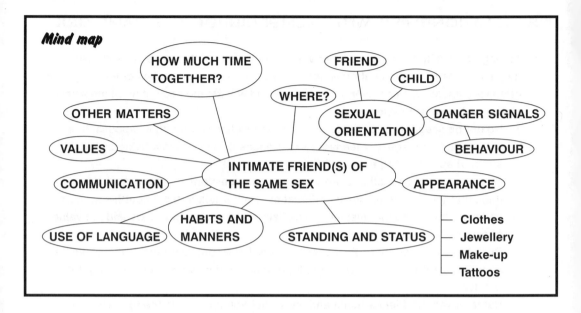

3. RELATIONSHIPS WITH OTHER INDIVIDUALS AND GROUPS

1. Your child's relationships with other individuals and groups, for example an older person, a teacher, coach, social group, sports friends and church group:
   - Because the child spends so much time with these persons and groups, parents are often concerned about the influence that they may have on him. There is also the feeling that I as parent am left out and no longer count except as provider of food and shelter. Grant your child this time, as it is important for developing inter-personal relationships and future socializing skills, problem-solving abilities, individuality and powers of discrimination (R1, R2, L2, L1).
   - Try to get to know the school friends and other friends he talks about so that you may judge for yourself who and what they are and which signs to look out for if you have doubts. Do not summarily criticize, disparage or belittle these friends. Try to say something good or interesting about them, otherwise they are going to avoid or ignore you in future (L1, R1).
   - Openly discuss your doubts with your child after giving the other party a fair chance. Leave it to his discretion whether he will continue the friendship (L1, R2).
   - Parents become worried about friendships with older persons (this can include a teacher or coach) especially if they smoke, enjoy a drink, take the child out, sometimes give him money, etc. Do not show that you have serious doubts about the person. Make opportunities to meet him, for example at your house, invite him to social functions, family outings and weekend visits. The other members of the family will soon make known their opinion so that you can test your own opinions or prejudices against theirs (L2, L1).
   - Talk to your child about that person. Ask why he likes him, what they talk about, where they go, why he isn't married, what his plans for the future are, what other friends he has. If you do it tactfully, the child will probably start gaining a broader

perspective and get over the stage of hero worship (L2, R1, R2).
- If your child wants to know why you are asking the questions, answer him honestly. Say that it is strange for an older person to have such a close friendship with a child and that there are so many examples of people abusing children. Tell him that you are concerned as a parent, but that you trust his judgement and good principles (R2).
- Do not hesitate to act or to summon help if you find that the friendship holds danger for your child. Always deal with it as objectively as possible (L2, R1).

2. My child's behaviour towards these individuals or groups:
   - Parents do not only look at who the persons or groups are with whom their children associate, they also look at how the child behaves and holds his own in these relationships.
   - Invite as many of his friends as possible to your home and get to know them so that you can make informed observations if you want to talk to your child about problems (L2, L1).
   - Attend as many group activities as your child allows you to, for example, sports practices and competitions, church camps, etc. Look at how he holds his own (L2, R1).
   - It is difficult to advise your child without him feeling that you are disparaging him. You must sometimes tactfully advise him on how to be more assertive with regard to his rights, "Don't you think you could insist a little more on ... It seems to me they get little more than their share ... Are you the only one who must clean up, pay so much ... " (R1).
   - Advise him tactfully on how to handle peer pressure and to maintain his principles (see **The generation gap**, p. 39) (L2).

3. School, weekend, holiday camps and school tours:
   - Parents often do not want their children to take part in these as one hears so many stories about things going wrong, especially if both sexes are involved. Children will also sometimes be more daring when they are in a group than when they are alone. However, we cannot begrudge them this opportunity to develop (R1).
   - Make sure what the aim of the outing is and discuss the advantages and disadvantages with your child. Will it be worth the time and money spent (especially if he has to pay part or all of the costs)? (L1, L2).
   - Make sure who are going on the outing and discuss it with your child. Ask questions such as: Do you like the children? Do you get along well? Aren't you going to be too lonely? Aren't they a little wild? (R2).
   - To forbid the child to go, usually won't solve the problem unless it is very clear that there may be trouble. Show therefore that you trust your child and believe that he will uphold his principles. Show that you are glad that he has the opportunity to enjoy himself and get wider experience (R2, R1).
   - Make sure what supervision there will be and which rules will apply. Discuss your doubts, if any, with the person who will supervise or the principal in a logical, objective way. Offer help where necessary, but your child should not get the idea that you want to spy on him (L1, L2).
   - Do not stand ready with countless "do's and don'ts" before they depart, especially not in front of his friends. Your child should know by this time what you want to say. Trust your upbringing and relax. Sigh audibly and say: "Oh, how nice to be young!"

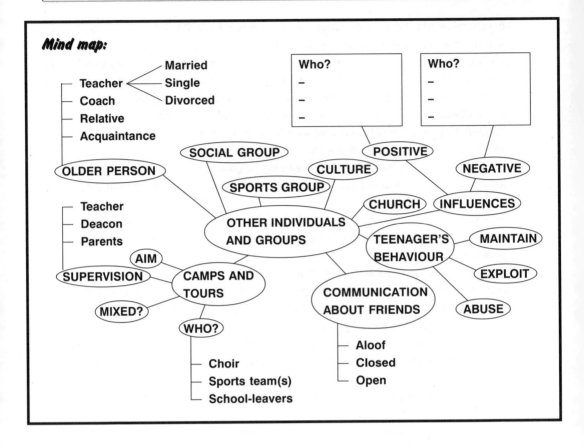

CONCLUSION

If smart parenting is our goal, we would do well to keep the following in mind:
- Let's spend quality time with our children. Let's get to know them as people in their own right and enjoy their humour and energy.
- Let's complain less and make fewer regulations, but draw up the rules in cooperation with our children and stick to them. Together we respect the rules, but also use the freedom within the rules. Therefore we need creativity.
- Let's say "us" instead of "you" more often so that everybody can become more involved and be empowered.
- Let's help them learn from the law of cause and effect instead of constant warnings. They will learn quickly that you will burn if you put your hand into the fire and will no longer need warnings.
- Let's withdraw from the threatening conflict and ask the child to come back later when he has calmed down, rather than feel that our honour is at stake and that we have to react equally vehemently.
- Let's separate the deed from the doer. Say the deed was bad, do not say the child is bad. We should also admit our own faults and create the attitude that these are learning opportunities.
- Let's always keep our long-term objectives in mind – how I want my child to

OTHER RELATIONSHIPS

act when he is an adult! Then I will think further than just to control the current situation as soon as possible.
- Let's try to be loving and firm at the same time. It brings respect. Love and respect work infectiously.
- Let's be consistent: what applies to the child, also applies to me with regard to behaviour, clothing, discipline, use of language, manners, work, play, etc. No double standards or hypocrisy!

Add some more of your own to the mind map (Feel free to consult the children!)

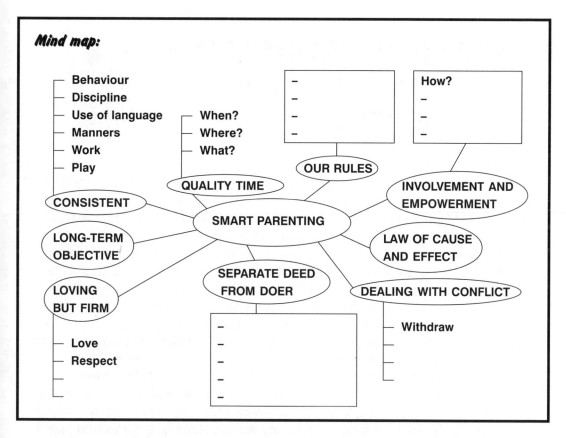

Enjoy your smart parenting and your smart teenager!

When Mother Theresa received her Nobel Prize, they asked her, "What can we do to promote world peace?" Her answer was, "Go home and love your family."

ENTREPRENEURSHIP

> *"What distinguishes the entrepreneur from the nonentrepreneur are initiative, an earnest desire to succeed, an ability to determine priorities, tenacity and persistence in the face of obstacles, and a willingness to get into action and still more action."*
>
> – Arthur C. Clarke –

18 ENTREPRENEURSHIP – ESSENTIAL IN THE 21ST CENTURY

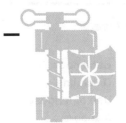

In South Africa, where the unemployment figure is approximately 30% and the economy does not grow quickly and strongly enough to create the necessary job opportunities, young people will, to an increasing extent, have to investigate and utilize self-employment possibilities and entrepreneurship.

Somebody has said that entrepreneurs are innovators who create demand. An entrepreneur is always on the lookout for new opportunities and challenges. He seizes these opportunities, develops unique products, obtains the necessary capital, brings about breakthroughs with regard to markets and processes, designs new technology, surprises with new designs, styles and ideas, rouses desires, fulfils eccentric needs. In the process he satisfies his own needs for success and creativity, makes money and creates job opportunities.

Most entrepreneurs are made, and it is here where the creative parent must see his role. It is a question of **recognizing** and **developing** talents. As in the case of any great sports and other achievements, success does not come automatically. Talent is important but to develop it optimally requires work, hard work! The parent can help the immature, inexperienced child to recognize and develop his talents, but particularly to **think** and **act** like an entrepreneur.

A culture of entrepreneurship must be created and encouraged in the parental home from an early age. Children must become disposed towards identifying opportunities, to think creatively and innovatively, generate ideas and concepts, to experiment, to look for hidden possibilities and consider alternatives. They must have the frankness to discuss it with their parents and share their dreams. Parents must understand the creative process, support the child's initiatives

ENTREPRENEURSHIP – ESSENTIAL IN THE 21ST CENTURY

with enthusiasm and make them develop further. Entrepreneurship must become a **way of life**.

Many children become dejected about the future when they realize that they will be one of thousands of school-leavers who must enter the labour market, where only one out of ten may get work. They must, therefore, consider starting their own small enterprise to create work for themselves. Here the parent has an im-portant role to keep them above-the-line thinkers and to help develop the qualities that will distinguish them as entrepreneurs.

There are certain worldwide trends of which parents must be aware and which they must keep bringing to their children's attention. Note the following:

- a new business is created every 8 seconds in the USA;
- the normal 40-hour per week worker is being replaced by temporary or contract workers or consultants – therefore temporary work is the route that must be followed to a full-time occupation;
- much of the work in a company is now done by specialists from outside or by machines. This creates many opportunities for workers who specialize in specific services.
  As specialists are more in demand than general workers, good technical skills and training are excellent assets;
- computers are indispensable in today's economy and their uses are expanded daily. Children must be made computer literate from as early an age as possible. They must also be trained to deal with the masses of information and to recognize opportunities.

CHARACTERISTICS OF ENTREPRENEURS

Research has shown that the following are the most important characteristics possessed or developed by entrepreneurs:

- a strong vision with regard to what they want to achieve;
- a positive self-image;
- belief in their own abilities;
- the ability to see and utilize opportunities;
- the ability to think creatively and conceptually;
- the ability to plan and the willpower to execute the plans of action;
- the ability to solve problems creatively and to make well-considered (whole-brain) decisions;
- the ability to take risks and deal with the consequences;
- good time management;
- passion and energy;
- a positive, future-orientated attitude towards life;
- good communication skills.

Which of these qualities do you think your child has, or has he developed? Tick them off. Remember, all of these characteristics can be acquired and developed.

> *"Nothing great has ever been reached without enthusiasm."*
> *— Ralph Waldo Emerson —*

PARENTS, THEIR BRAIN PREFERENCES AND POSSIBLE REACTIONS TO THE IDEA OF ENTREPRENEURSHIP

> *"Success is the result if you do what you want to do. There is no other way to be successful."*
>
> – Malcolm Forbes –

We are now going to discuss each of the four brain quadrants with the emphasis on their thinking preferences with regard to entrepreneurship. Look at your dominant quadrant. That is where your strongest priorities will lie, although not all of the processes will necessarily apply to you, while some of the characteristics described under your secondary and tertiary quadrants, will. Your approach to entrepreneurship will influence your interaction with your child and his preferences in this regard.

THE L1 PARENT

- You will probably have a logical, rational approach to your child's future. Therefore you will expect him to know from an early age what he wants to do one day and train himself for it;
- to this end he must already choose his school subjects in such a way that he can have practical, technical or academical tertiary training;
- you will probably let him take aptitude and career-orientated tests and make a thorough study of his brain preferences;
- you may underestimate or disparage the creative, the experimental and quest for alternatives as unrealistic and a waste of time. In so doing you will disregard the essence of entrepreneurship. On account of your superior knowledge and experience, you may tend to want to choose for him, instruct and sometimes even force him in a certain direction;
- his indecision or fears about the future may irritate you, because you think realistically and are performance-driven;
- whether he makes enough money may be an issue to you, because you know what the cost of living is;
- you will tend to provide your child with a great deal of concrete information

about occupations and occupational fields, and will also spell out their respective advantages and disadvantages;
- you will probably try to influence your child to take only calculated risks.

THE L2 PARENT

- You will have a practical, structured approach and will want the child to prepare himself systematically for his future;
- because you are task-oriented, you want him to decide early on what he wants to become or do and acquire and practise the necessary skills for it – practical, technical or academical – so that he will be able to do it well;
- you will probably let him take aptitude, career-orientated and skills tests and give high priority to his brain preferences;
- you may also underestimate the creative, the experimental and the quest for alternatives, writing them off as impractical and nonconstructive thinking. In so doing you will disregard the essence of entrepreneurship;
- you may expect him to visit work places and professional people to gain first-hand knowledge about the occupations that interest him (possibly you). You may even expect him to work there during holidays in order to gain experience;
- you may expect him to produce concrete plans for the future which contain few inherent risks;
- you will expect him to choose a career or job which offers security so that you will not have to worry about him and his future family;
- you may be concerned about the safety and health aspects of the work that he has in mind.

THE R2 PARENT

- You will understand the child's fears and uncertainties and try to reassure him. Be careful not to give him false reassurance that can lead to a *laissez-faire* attitude;
- you may also tend to overreact if you become worried because he still does not know where he is going and then constantly nag him about it;
- you will probably make him take aptitude and personality tests and try to understand his brain preferences;
- you will encourage him to investigate the creative, the experimental and the development of alternatives and to further his skills in those fields. In so doing you will support the essence of entrepreneurship;
- you will probably encourage him to have work holidays first, to travel and do piece-work so that he can become emotionally more mature before he makes a final decision about his future;
- you will encourage him to talk to people who have made a success of their

career, let him attend motivation seminars, point out role models and make available to him information about successful entrepreneurs;
- you will not be concerned about how much money he will make one day, but rather whether he will be happy and make an honest living;
- you may be concerned about the hours that he will work, his health, the influence of his job on his personal life and the people close to him (for example his marriage and family).

THE R1 PARENT

- You may have a holistic, future-oriented approach. You will observe the trends in the labour market and point out where the possibilities and opportunities lie (create scenarios);
- you probably won't expect your child to know at an early age what he wants to do one day; he must rather keep his options, his eyes and thinking open;
- you will promote a positive attitude about the future and counter negative talk or problem-directed thinking by searching for new possibilities;
- you will actively promote the creative, the experimental and the quest for alternatives and in so doing support the essence of entrepreneurship;
- you will insist on creativity, personality, skill and aptitude tests. The individual thinking preferences emphasized by brain profiles will especially interest you;
- you will encourage your child to visit a great variety of work places and entrepreneurs and make his own observations;
- you will encourage him to attend seminars, creativity and skills workshops, watch interesting videos, read books and magazines and go on outings with a view to discovering interesting careers;
- you will help him do strategic planning;
- you will not necessarily worry about how much money he will earn, but whether the career is likely to expand in the future, whether he will be able to diversify and stay in demand;
- you will not really be worried about his hard work and the demands set by his career, but whether he will experience passion and excitement;
- you will encourage him to be ready to take risks.

20 THE TEENAGER'S BRAIN PREFERENCES AND ENTREPRENEURSHIP

> *"Dream great dreams; dare great hopes. Have great expectations; dare great expectations."*
>
> — Norman Vincent Peale —

There are again eleven brain profiles, from which you must pick the one which is closest to that of your child. Keep in mind what you have already learnt about combination preferences and be selective. Also remember that not all of the preferences of a specific quadrant will necessarily apply to him.

A number of occupational fields are given which are typical of the particular profile. The child may want to practise entrepreneurship in some of these fields. We refer to the variety of possible occupations within the field and sometimes also the skills required for success in them. These only serve as examples to stimulate your thoughts and are by no means complete. The idea is that parent and child should further investigate the possibilities together.

The parent's task is to support the child in his decision-making and the development of specific skills. You must always listen with interest, react positively and supportively and encourage him to look for new opportunities and fields within those mentioned as well as the countless other occupations that exist. **He must especially look with fresh eyes for occupational possibilities in the 21st century.**

Mind maps are also given to help you support the child when he considers a certain field. These are examples of how to develop an overall picture. Let him strongly visualize the need(s) within a particular occupational field, then conjure up a product or service in his imagination that will provide in that need and then write down various possibilities for further consideration. These mind maps are not complete, so that you and your child can expand on them. We want to emphasize once again that the lists of occupations are merely strong indications of the extensive choice and possibilities that exist. Add to them with your child.

L1 PROFILE

- He is analytical, precise and likes to work with facts
- he can look at things objectively and reason logically
- he is focussed and performance-oriented

Occupational fields
- **Economic and financial**
- analyse markets, products and services, marketing of products and services
- do computer programming (also with regard to the above) buy and sell hard and software, train people in computer programming
- operate an Internet café for training, information, recreation, e-mail
- do financial analyses, manage client's finances, general financial management and control, training
- e-mail analyses
- analyse Internet trends.

- **Domestic and industrial**
- What can make people's work easier? Analyse different types of work and the existing services and resources. Then create new ones, for example for the housewife, farmer, factory worker, doctor and minister
- consumer research

- **Science**

Research in several fields aimed at, amongst others:
- cultivating new products, for example agricultural vegetation
- developing new medicines and insecticides
- designing new resources and implements
- making artificial limbs and other medical aids for diseased and injured people.

- **Law and labour relations**
- lawyers, advocates
- gather, interpret, disseminate information
- guidance with regard to rights, interpretation of laws.

- **Technology**
- improvement of existing technical resources in every possible field, for example cellular phones, e-mail and other means of telecommunication.

What occupations and occupational fields can you add for the LJ person?

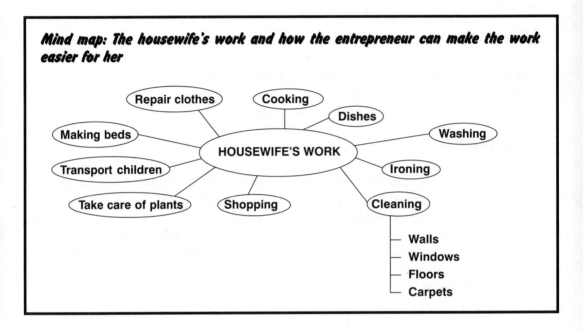

Possibilities, after looking at the brain card:
- 1-hour housecleaning service, window washing, carpets and furniture cleaning, painting and small repairs
- food order and delivery service, health-food packages for meals and school children
- pre-cooked vegetables, stew
- clothing repairs service; collect, wash, iron and deliver laundry
- collect, wash and iron curtains and hang them again
- provide small water purification systems for the kitchen
- plant exchange service
- shopping service
- transport service for children to and from school and extra-mural activities
- after-school help and supervision service, sports and other types of coaching.

What other creative ideas do you have?

L2 PROFILE

- He is systematic, categorized, organized
- he likes security, routine, rules and regulations
- he is practical and task-oriented

Occupational fields
- **Administration**
- design computer programs to facilitate procedures and ensure better control
- build and repair computers; install systems and networks
- improve filing systems
- install and operate databases; collect, process and disseminate information
- administer funds, bursaries, sports clubs, other clubs and organizations.

- **Technology and mechanics**
- do motor mechanics and design
- repair and improve electronic apparatus, devices
- recycle paper, plastic, cans and bottles. Create new products such as containers, packaging material, writing paper
- install machinery, conveyor belt systems
- plumber, fitter and turner
- electro-technical and mechanical engineering projects

- **Nursing**
- hospital, clinic and private nursing services
- develop new nursing techniques and resources

- **Planning and management**
- situation analysis
- compiling budgets
- plans of action
- project management

Of what other occupations and occupational fields for the L2 person can you think?

Mind map: Recycling of used products and manufacturing new ones

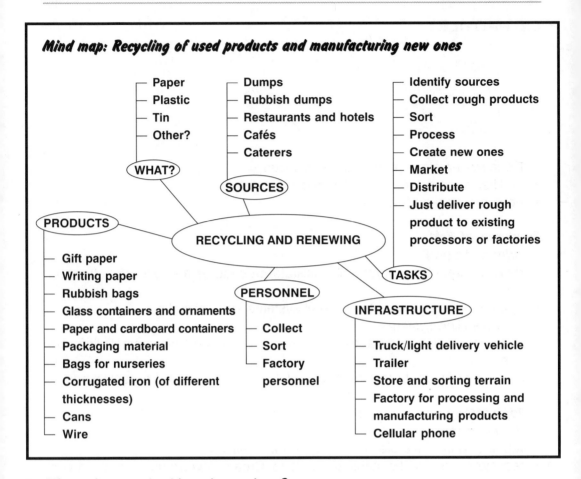

What other creative ideas do you have?

R2 PROFILE

- He is emotional, sensitive, empathetic
- he likes people, interaction and teamwork
- he likes communication and is people-oriented

Occupational fields
- **Teaching, training and education**
- human resources development
- design better educational methods, new syllabuses, outcomes-based programmes, coaching methods, life skills
- whole-brain education and coaching
- motivation and self-development
- children supervision business
- develop recreational opportunities.

- **Communication**
- improve communication skills and approach
- renew communication systems such as e-mail, cellular phones and use of Internet
- improve public relations
- undertake and teach others about negotiation and dealing with conflict.

- **Marketing**
- verbal, written and other marketing of products and services
- estate agent
- sales agent

- **Social**
- find ways and design aids to help people, especially in communities, to improve their quality of living
- to make the world and way of living easier for the disabled, the injured, the elderly and the ill
- provide assistance with regard to combating crime, drug addiction, Aids and other social problems
- therapeutic directions.

- **Tourism**
- introduce new, interesting places to visit, locally and overseas, to the public or travel agencies
- arrange sight-seeing tours – birds, animals, plants, flowers, insects, butterflies
- tour operator, tour guide.

- **Consultation and guidance**
- psychological or social services
- education and training (outside the school)
- motivation and self-development (outside the school)

Of what other occupations and occupational fields for the R2 person can you think?

Mind map: Public relations

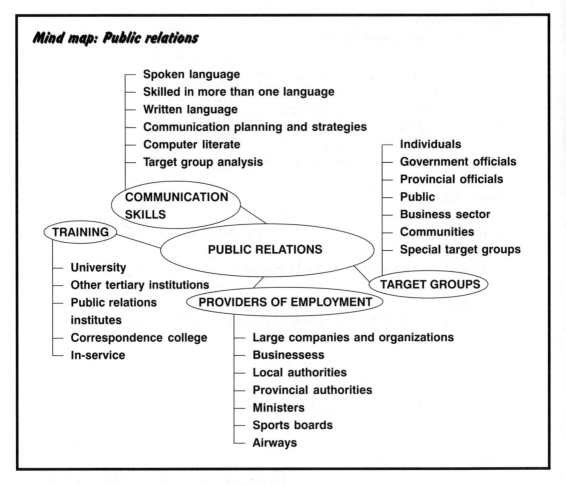

What other creative ideas do you have?

R1 PROFILE

- He is holistic, future-orientated, strategic
- he likes to work with concepts and ideas
- he compiles something new (synthesis) after experiments and his quest for alternatives

Occupational fields

- **Strategic planning**
- see trends for the future and create scenarios
- plan with a view to future impact.

- **Advertising**
- visualize and produce strong visual portrayal of things
- generate original ideas and concepts
- write, draw, sketch, compose, orchestrate
- develop video and audio programmes for companies.

- **Architect**
- 3-dimensional, visual ability
- seek aesthetic satisfaction.

- **Landscape architect and gardening**
- garden lay-out, aesthetic, creative, individual tastes
- caring for garden – knowledge of ground, plants, climate, feeding, etc.
- Designing of special focal points such as fountains, ponds, waterfalls, rock gardens, etc.

- **Interior decorating**
- conduct interviews and establish individual needs
- visual and aesthetic impact
- give advice, improvise.

- **Fine and performing arts**
- sculpting, pottery, painting, etc.
- Drama, theatre, dancing, singing, music, puppet show
- graphic design, composing, theatrical set design.

- **Tourism**
- discover and create new places to visit, entertainment
- guest houses, hotels, restaurants, pubs
- satisfying a large variety of individual needs and tastes.

- **Education and training**
- designing of courses in many fields for the requirements of the 21st century
- project occupations of the future.

Of what other occupations and occupational fields for the R1 person can you think?

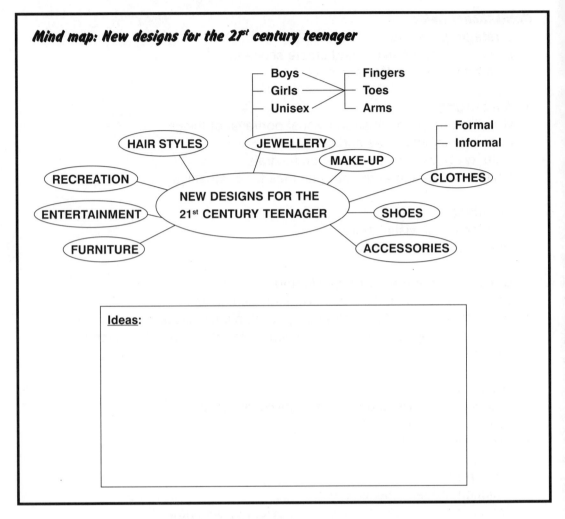

Mind map: New designs for the 21st century teenager

Ideas:

What other creative ideas do you have?

L1-L2 PROFILE

- He gives preference to analytical thinking, factual argument and a rational approach

- he prefers categorized, organized and practical processes
- he is performance and task-oriented

Occupational fields
- **Systems analysis, design, building and installation**
- computer systems and networks for businesses, factories, organizations and houses according to individual preferences and needs
- safety systems
- computer programs for planning, organization, control, financial analysis, general management, etc.
- Production systems from raw material to final product.

Market analyses and product development (see brain card).

- **Economic**
- manage investment portfolios after thorough analysis.

- **Mechanic and civil engineering**
- establishment and maintenance of infrastructures in rural and urban communities

- **Instrument technician**
- analyse problems and needs and make the necessary instruments and implements, e.g. in research, manufacturing, measuring and evaluation.

- **Tooth technician**
- make fillings, constructions, artificial teeth, implantations to provide in unique needs.

- **Acquisition manager**
- analyse the market and determine the demand
- analyse and compare prices
- control and confirm acquisition and stores.

Of what other occupations and occupational fields for the L1-L2 person can you think?

Mind map: Market analysis and product development

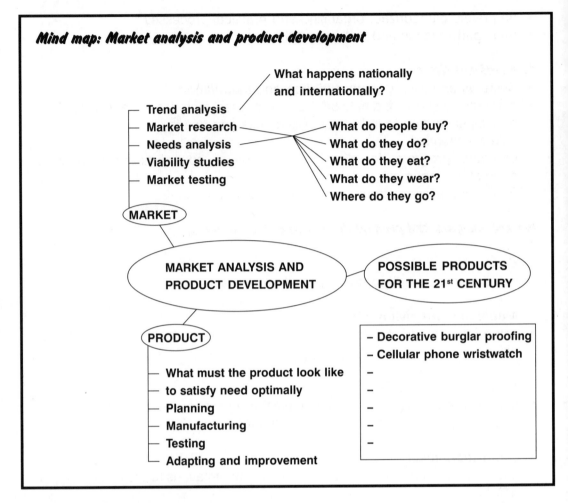

What other creative ideas do you have?

L2-R2 PROFILE

- He gives preference to the practical, ordered, structured processes
- he likes interaction with people, communication and is comfortable with emotions

- he combines task and person orientation

Occupational fields
- **Training and coaching**
- Convey technical skills with regard to computers, instruments, implements
- Teach physical skills as in sports coaching, physical development, physiotherapy and occupational therapy
- general life skills

- **Delivery and distribution services**
- Do needs determination and identify rivals already providing these services
- Marketing and market development
- communication, organization and control
- physical labour.

- **Arranging and organizing social and work functions**
- market services for arranging all types of functions such as weddings, cocktail parties, conferences
- liaise with clients, arrange suitable places and rooms
- determine needs with regard to catering, menu, apparatus
- negotiate, provide, transport, determine prices, tender.

- **Communication**
- write communication plans and strategies.

Of what other occupations and occupational fields for the L2-R2 person can you think?

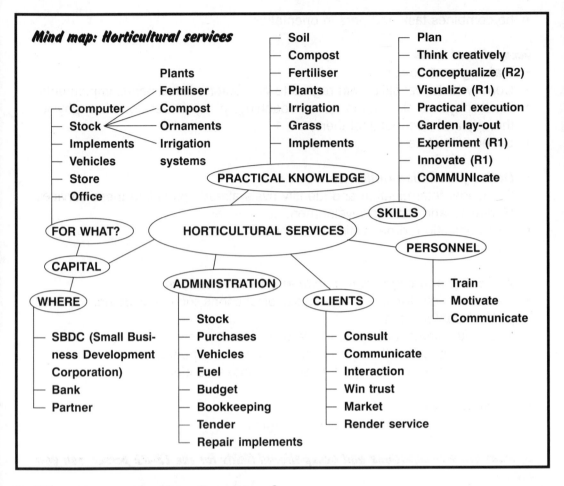

What other creative ideas do you have?

R2-R1 PROFILE

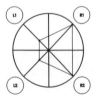

- He prefers people, interaction, communication and feelings
- he is very comfortable with change, new concepts and ideas, experimenting and innovation
- he is both people and future-oriented

Occupational fields
- *Manager or owner of hotel, guest house, restaurant (see mind map).*
- *Marketing*
- Produce new marketing initiatives for ideas, products and services such as advertisements, videos, photo series, puppet show, shows.

- *Tourism*
- Provide new places to visit, experiences, entertainment, fun
- rendering of service, satisfying of needs, caring
- communication, atmosphere, empathy.

- *Education*
- Present courses in design, creative arts, psychology, motivation and languages
- course and curriculum design for the 21st century.

Of what other occupations and occupational fields for the R2-R1 person can you think?

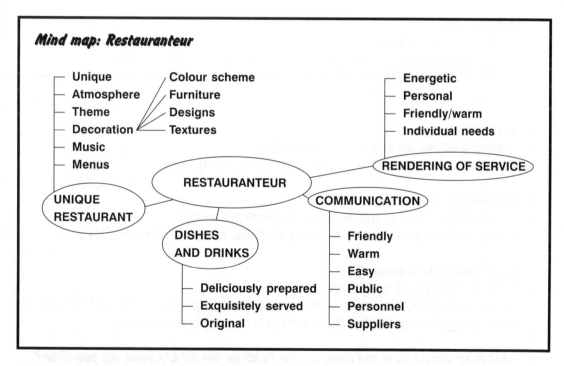

What other creative ideas do you have?

R1-L1 PROFILE

- He gives preference to ideas, concepts, experimentation, holistic thinking
- he is also analytical, logical, objective and rational
- he is, therefore, both future and performance-oriented

Occupational fields
- **Finances**
- do financial analyses and forecasts
- invest (risk) on stock-market.

- **Medical**
- diagnose illnesses
- paediatrics

- **Advertising**
- analyse clients' needs
- analyse great variety of target markets and their specific needs
- create advertisements for products such as motor cars, groceries as well as services.

- **Product design**
- market analysis and needs determination
- design product for viable market, e.g. computer games

- **Rendering of service**
- needs determination and analysis of existing services
- create suitable service and auxiliary facilities, such as Internet cafés.

- **Education and training**
- analyse needs and target market
- design suitable courses for every need which may arise in the 21st century, such as development of skills or computerized sports coaching.

Of what other occupations and occupational fields for the R1-L1 person can you think?

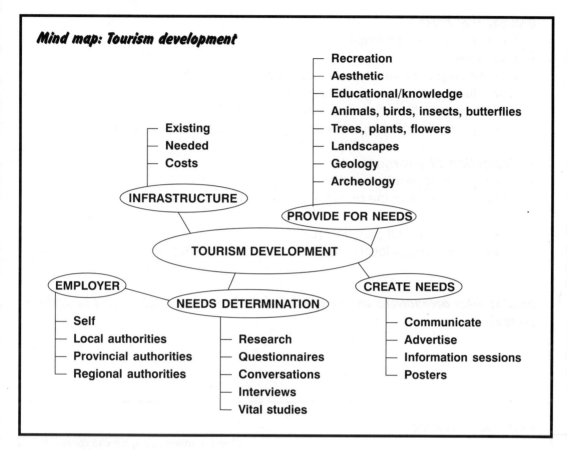

Mind map: Tourism development

What other creative ideas do you have?

THE VERSATILE L1-L2-R2-R1 PROFILE

- He does not show specific strong preferences
- he has preferences in all the quadrants
- he is reasonably performance and task-oriented, as well as people and future-oriented

Occupational fields

- **Librarian** (see mind map).
- **Publisher**
- analyse target markets for a variety of publications (L1)
- typesetting and language editing (L2)
- communicate with writers, personnel, public (R2)
- develop creative covers, attractive displays, satisfy individual tastes (R1).

- **Protection of environment**
- holistic view of problem and/or threat (R1)
- intensive analysis of the distribution, environment and characteristics of species (L1)
- research and careful planning (L2)
- communication with local authorities, provincial authorities, public, individuals (R2).

Of what other occupations and occupational fields can you think for this versatile person?

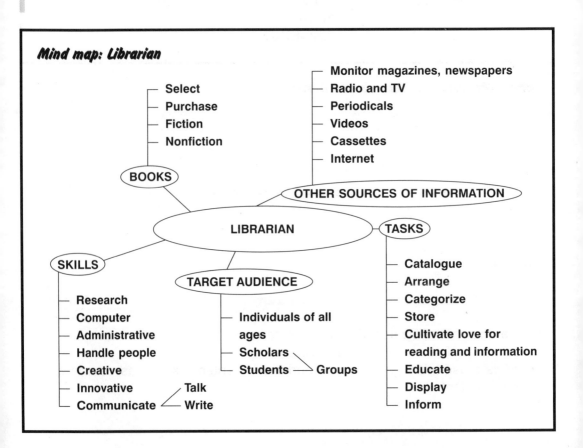

What other creative ideas do you have?

L1-R2 PROFILE

- He is realistic, logical, analytical and rational
- he is also people-oriented, empathic, likes interaction and communicates well
- he is therefore both performance and people oriented and will want to apply his analytical, logical abilities in the best interests of people

Occupational fields
- **Financial consultant (see mind map).**
- **Education and training**
- instruction in computer science, mathematics, physical science, chemistry, biology
- instruction in financial management, economy, market analysis
- instruction in various subject methodologies

- **Medical**
- general practitioner, radiologist, surgeon
- dentist, oral hygienist

- **Journalism**
- financial journalist

- **Commercial pilot**

Of what other occupations and occupational fields for the L1-R2 person can you think?

smart PARENTS

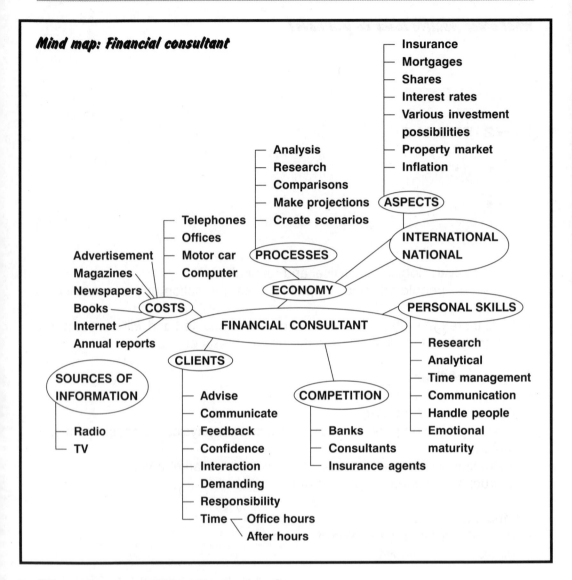

What other creative ideas do you have?

R1-L2 PROFILE

- He is conceptual, innovative, likes to take risks and to experiment
- he is also practical, ordered, likes to organize
- he is both task and future-oriented

Occupational fields
- **Strategic planning**
- creating scenarios for the future
- systematic planning of strategies for the future

- **Sculptor or painter**
- conceptualizing and visualization
- systematic, practical approach

- **Designer**
- holistic, 3-dimensional capabilities
- systematic, detailed drawing and reproduction

- **Chef**
- likes experimenting
- exquisite preparation and serving
- step-by-step, systematic preparation and cooking
- purchase and control of stock

- **Theatre: building of sets**
- total image of set
- artistic feeling
- step-by-step construction
- aesthetic, but practical – quick to erect and change, multi-purpose cost-effective.

Of what other occupations and occupational fields can you think for the R1-L2 person?

Mind map: Taking care of and entertaining children (R1, L2 and R2)

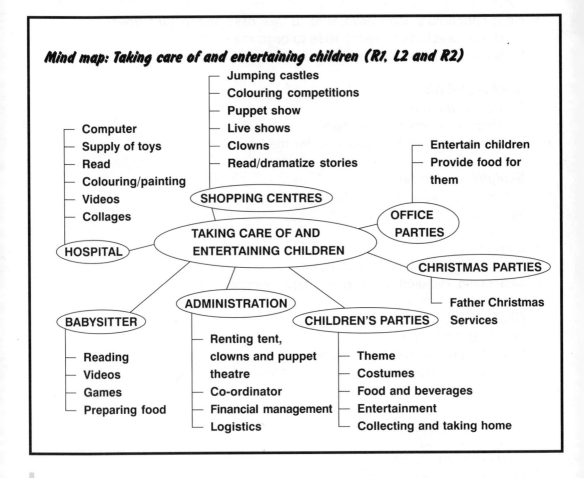

What other creative ideas do you have?

THINK AND DO: DEVELOP A BUSINESS PLAN

> *"Enthusiasm is the sparkle in your eye, the hop in your step, the grabbing of your hand, the irresistible welling up of the will and energy to execute your ideas."*
>
> — Walter Crysler —

When your child has now looked with fresh eyes at the above and enthusiastically started generating ideas and concepts, he may have the "aha" experience and produce an interesting, sometimes brilliant money-making idea. It is now time to approach it in whole-brain fashion to ensure success. Encourage him to follow the following steps by answering the questions:

- Can you very strongly visualize the need, as well as the product that will satisfy the need? If you can, write down the possibilities (R1).
- Who is going to need your product or service? Analyse your target market carefully, for example toddlers, teenagers, the elderly, the general public (L1).
- How often are they going to need it? Make a thorough study of how large the market is, is it seasonal, will there be a constant demand for it (L1, L2)?
- What will they pay for it? Make sure that the product or service is affordable for the specific target market. The costs that you will incur to produce the product or render the service will naturally have to be calculated very carefully (L1, L2).
- Who are your competitors? How strong is the competition? What will you do to eliminate or outshine the competition (L1, R1)?
- What are your short and long-term objectives? Be very specific and write them down (L2, R1).
- When do you want to reach these objectives? Write down the dates and action steps that you will have to take (R1, L2).
- Where are you going to manufacture your product or render your service? Is it the best place? Why (L1)?
- Do you have the necessary capital to start your project? If not, where are you going to seek help? How will you convince the person or persons to help you (R2)?
- Who will be involved in the project? Make sure that you are clear about everyone's role, responsibilities, duties and remuneration before you start (R2, L2).
- How will you effectively make your target market aware of your service or

product? Are there costs involved? Did you bring them into account (R1, R2, L1)?
- How will you keep book of your income and expenditure to make sure that your business is making a profit (L2)?
- Did you establish whether you need a licence to run your business (L2)?

CONCLUSION

If you have worked attentively through this section about entrepreneurship, if you have reconsidered your child's talents and brain preferences, as well as your own approach to entrepreneurship, which will now definitely be a whole-brain approach, you should be ready to help your child to think and act like an entrepreneur. You will be able to develop in him a whole-brain approach to occupations and occupational fields, especially by doing mind maps and expanding existing mind maps. You will be able to help him look for new opportunities and possibilities, to think innovatively and future-oriented and to reconcile the conceptual with the practical. As an above-the-line parent you will have above-the-line children who will not face the future, like thousands of others of their age, with fear, but with self-confidence and passion.

Allow entrepreneurship to become a way of life in your home!

> *"There is no security on this earth. There is only opportunity."*
> *— Gen. Douglas MacArthur —*

A child's future does not just happen, it is created!

SMART PARENTS IS A SERIES OF **FOUR BOOKS**.

THE FIRST BOOK IN THE SERIES IS A WORK-BOOK FOR PARENTS:
SMART PARENTS ... CHILDREN AND TEENAGERS

IN ADDITION TO THE WORK-BOOK FOR *teenagers*, A FURTHER TWO WORK-BOOKS (FOR PARENTS AND THEIR CHILDREN) ARE AVAILABLE, WHICH TARGET SPECIFIC AGE GROUPS:

preschoolers
children (primary school)

ORDER THESE BOOKS IN THE SERIES FROM CARPE DIEM:

(016) 982-3617